Call Upon Me

Call Upon Me

*About the practise
of our prayer*

H. Westerink

Published by the I.L.P.B.
London, Ontario, Canada

RESPONSE TO YOUR BAPTISM

Translated from ROEP MIJ AAN
by Mr. H. Westerink

Translated by Elizabeth Englefield
Edited by Rob Schouten

Printed with permission from
UITGEVERIJ DE VUURBAAK, BARNEVELD

Published by the I.L.P.B.
London, Ontario, Canada
Box 783   N6A 4Y8

ISBN 088666 014 9

Foreword

The late Rev. J. van Bruggen in his 'Aantekeningen bij the Heidelbergse Cathechismus' wrote this about prayer: "Although prayer is indeed 'the breath of the soul' and we cannot do without it any less than we can do without our breath, prayer does not come about in the life of a Christian by itself. Prayer is a holy art which we need to learn time and again."

In this book Mr. Westerink examines not only what Scriptures say about prayer but also our attitudes and obligations towards prayer. He makes it abundantly clear that indeed "prayer is a holy art which we need to learn". When I was proofreading the manuscript, time and time again I became so involved with the content that I forgot I was proofreading. Mr. Westerink's unceasing appeal to the Scriptures makes prayer unfold before us in all its power and comfort and the relationship it grants us with our Father to who we may and must send up our prayers.

It is the sincere desire of the I.L.P.B. that the reader may draw on this book for comfort and stimulation.

A sincere thanks goes out to all who have assisted in the publication of the book.

Tolle Lege   For the I.L.P.B.

C. Hoff

Introduction

This book deals with personal prayer.

It deals with the difficulties we can have with prayer; with the blessing it may be to ourselves and to others and with the glory God may receive in it.

It seeks to do this simply, as in a talk between believers. Above all it seeks to do this in a Scriptural way. In connection with this I should mention the references. There are rather a lot of them. The idea is not that every reader should check them all, since that would hinder reading. The intention is that any reader, whenever he or she feels the need to, can fall back on the actual Word of God. For not human words, but only God's Word can make our prayer life flourish. Only God's Word can do that.

God's Word teaches us to pray.

Contents

Introduction

Foreword

Prayer at bottom is committing oneself to God
Prayer is to acknowledge in faith, God as he is
Prayer is an active self expression to the Father
and a simultaneous, conscious attachment
*   of the self to the Judge.*
To pray is to put oneself in the right position
*   overagainst God.*

Dr. K. Schilder

1 Prayer

When we pray we speak to God.

We enter into the heavenly sanctuary. There we place ourselves before God's throne. And we address Him, God Himself, on the basis of promises He Himself has given us, and in the firm confidence that He listens to us.

Prayer is that mighty.

Indispensable

Inst.3 20:2

In his Institutes Calvin says that through prayer the treasures of God's promises are uncovered and won. And further he says that through prayer we draw near to the Lord, that He may indeed grant us His presence and help.

Prayer has been called the breathing of our spiritual life. And the Lord Jesus compares it with a child *Matt.7:7-12* knocking at a door and asking for bread. Prayer is that indispensable in the life with the Lord.

Beyond prayer and contemplation

Praying is so simple that a small child can and may do it: Lord, bless this food. Amen.

It is also so difficult that adults in all their life are never finished with it: Lord, teach us to pray.

1

It is so powerful that we may do it in all circumstances and for all needs.

Do we actually do this?

A young man was unable to find a girlfriend, and as a result he became lonely and despondent. He discussed the matter with his minister, who asked him: Have you ever prayed about this? No, never. He had never put this need before God's throne.

Someone complained about the sermons of his minister. He had listened to them for several years, Sunday after Sunday, but had not received any benefit from them, he said. Finally he came to talk to the minister.

Again the question: Did you pray about it?

And again the reply: No, never.

Not for himself; not for the church; not for the minister.

Ps 81:10

Were these people unbelievers? Certainly not. But in their prayer life they were below the level God has established. He said: "Open your mouth wide, and I will fill it." He makes that word come true, beyond prayer and contemplation.

Many of God's children can testify to this.

Prayer in occupied territory

John 12:31

We live and pray in territory occupied by the ruler of this world; Satan.

In this world we are no heroes of prayer.

The devil has to make but a small effort and our trust in the Lord is no longer highly charged.

Heb. 12:15

So easily we come short of the grace of God.

2

Then our prayer does not come off the ground very easily; it may not even go up at all.

There is a great danger that we simply acquiesce in that and think that life with the Lord has little joy and little result.

Phil.4:6-7   When we read, then, that in everything we may by prayer and supplication with thanksgiving let our requests be made known to God, and that then the peace of God which passes all understanding will keep our hearts and minds in Christ Jesus-then- in all honesty, we are disappointed.

Is this supposed to be that peace of God, this, which we feel and experience?

Call upon Me

And it is a good thing too, if at least we are disappointed, for that means we still have higher expectations. For faith can never expect too much. But life through that faith, also prayer life, doesn't just come to us. It demands our efforts.

1 Tim. 4:7   "Train yourself in godliness."
1 Thes. 5:17   "Pray without ceasing."
Ps. 50:15A   *"Call upon Me* in the day of trouble... "

Mark 10:47,48   *Call,* in the way that Bartholomew did - as a blind beggar at the roadside: "Have mercy on me!"

Then we take a deep breath.

Then we urgently knock at God's door.

Then we draw the Lord near to us.

We dig *out* the treasures of His promises.

Luke 11:1   "Lord, teach us to pray."

3

2 The Living God

Ps.42:3

There are those who can testify:
"My soul thirsts for God."
What they read in psalm 27 comes straight from their hearts:

Ps.27:8-9

"Thou hast said, 'Seek ye My face'. "
My heart says to Thee,
"Thy face, LORD, do I seek."
Hide not Thy face from me...

Ps.31:17

But on their calling they do not experience God's face shining upon them in love. Their thirst for God is not quenched.

Why not?

The true God

The first question they should ask themselves is this: Do I really call upon *God*? The *true* God?

Or did I get caught in Satan's snare?

There are people who still really believe in "something", a ruling higher power. But who can call upon a blind power and have peace?

Others believe that there is a supreme being. They arrange all beings in a line: plants, animals, people, spirits... In sequence they are each one on a higher level. And at the top they picture the supreme being. That is their god. But such a being, even such

4

a supreme being, is limited. God is no "higher power". Neither is He a "supreme being", on the same line with other beings.

He is *God!*

Now we should not think that such ideas cannot harm us, in the belief that we know better after all.

Eph.6:12   For the spiritual hosts of wickedness in the air can also contaminate us with such ideas, even in a "christian" way. How?

By our thinking of God as if He were a dogma, a doctrine which we have in our minds.

We speak no evil of dogma here. We may not denigrate the doctrines of the church, as is sometimes done even by believers. We must know the dogmas well and teach them to our children, also those dogmas in which the church speaks with reverence about God.

1 Tim.4:6   And the church must teach the *doctrine.*

1 Tit.2:7   Titus had to be a model of purity in doctrine.

And what then does Scripture teach us? And what does dogma teach us? This, that God is the *living* God.

The living God

That is how He has revealed Himself. And that is how we may know and love Him.

1 Sam.17:36   Goliath was slain because he had defied the armies of the living God.

David derived strength from the knowledge:
Ps. 18:36   *"The LORD lives."*
Is. 63:9   He sympathizes with His people:

5

"In all their affliction He was afflicted."
We may address Him, and then He *sees* and *hears*:

Ps. 94:9
"He who planted the ear, does He not hear?
"He who formed the eye, does He not see?"

When we cry to Him, His *heart* is moved with compassion for us:

Hosea 11:8
"How can I give you up, O Ephraim? How
can I hand you over, O Israel! How can I
make you like Adamah! How can I treat you
like Zeboim! My heart recoils within Me, My
compassion grows warm and tender."

He has *pity* on us:

Ps.103:13
"As a father pities his children,
so the LORD pities those who fear Him."

He who calls upon Him does not call into empty space.

For He *is* there to listen to us. We can depend on Him.

We can flee to Him. On the wave length of His promises we may address Him.

We can give ourselves to Him- our troubles, our questions, our sorrows and our joys. We can take them to Him, and leave them with Him. With Him they are in good hands.

Is.50:2
"Is My hand shortened, that it cannot
redeem? Or have I no power to deliver?"

Living by the Scriptures

But then we will have to come to Him, the true, the living God.

If we do not want to be caught in Satan's snares we must listen carefully to God, as He speaks to us in the Scriptures.

We must not turn to our self-made image of Him, or to a dogma.

Ps.103:10

For certainly it is true that God is merciful, also with respect to our prayers. He does not deal with us according to our sins.

This, however, does not give us the liberty to think of Him any way we see fit. We may not have a god before Him that we have made up for ourselves, nor bow to such a god and call upon it. For then our words of prayer fall back upon ourselves -like rocks. Only he who calls on the *living* God finds a listening ear and a merciful heart!

Ps.116:2

"He inclined His ear to me,
therefore I will call on Him
as long as I live."

7

3 The Holy God

The living God is also the *holy* God.

What does that mean? What does it mean for our prayer?

Shouldn't God's holiness frighten us? Doesn't it put a damper on our prayer?

Where will our feet stand?

Holy, that is: highly exalted. *So* high and *so* exalted that it is beyond our imagination. All we can really do is stammer: God is GOD, God who is immeasurable by any means and impossible to classify.

Is 40:25
> *"To whom then will you compare Me, that I should be like him? says the Holy One."*

Job 34:37
Job 24:12
Job 27: 2
Job had to learn what these words mean for man. He multiplied his words against God. The LORD, Job said, would not pay attention to the prayer of the dying and wounded. Job thought He had taken away his rights.

Is.40:26
Then the Holy One, who "has created all these", put Job in his place:

Job 40:2
> *"Shall a faultfinder contend with the Almighty?*

Job 38:4
> *Where were you when I laid the foundation of the earth?*

8

Job 38:12

Have you commanded the morning since your days began, and caused the dawn to know its place?"

Job 40:4,5

And Job lay his hand on his mouth:
"I have spoken once, and I will not answer; twice, but I will proceed no further."
So exalted is God in His holiness.

Gen 18:27

And we, we are dust and ashes. How shall we enter into His high place and address Him personally?

That question becomes more pressing yet. For distance between God and man is not necessarily enmity. In the garden of Eden God walked with Adam and Eve, and it was good.

But when we hear the word *holy*, what do we think of first of all?

Deut.32:4
PS.92:15
Ps.5:5

Is it not of *blamelessness*, the absence of sin? And indeed, in that too God is highly exalted, for all His ways are just. There is no unrighteousness in Him. Wickedness does not delight Him and evil will not sojourn with Him.

1 Pet.1:16

"You shall be holy, for I am holy."

And this places a baricade on the way to God. For *we* are not holy.

Ps. 51:5

We are born in iniquity.

Rom.3:10

In sin our mothers have conceived us. Not one of us is righteous, no, not one. And the mind that is set on the flesh-that is, what we have become because of sin-is hostile to God; it is ungodliness and wickedness. We cannot be more unholy than that.

Rom.8:7

This is no trifling matter. We can not lightly skip over it, thinking that the Holy One will overlook it too. How then can we gain admittance to the throne of God? Where in His holy place would we put our

9

Is.6:1-5

feet so that we might address Him? Shouldn't we, like Isaiah, who saw the LORD seated on His high and exalted throne, who heard the seraphim call: "Holy, holy, holy is the LORD of hosts", shouldn't we also say: Woe is me! For I am lost, for I am a man, a woman, of unclean lips?

And with that, hasn't prayer become impossible?

The covenant uniting us with God

This would indeed be the case if God in His great mercy had not revealed *more* about His holiness. But He has in fact done so. For He is holy not only in that He is almighty. He is highly exalted not only in that no unrighteousness is found in Him. He is also holy and highly exalted in His love, in His compassion, in His mercy, in His faithfulness. He is always the Holy One, incomparable; His ways are always to the benefit of His people.

After the fall into sin, Adam and Eve hid from the LORD God.

Gen.3:9

The child hid from his Father. Then the Father Himself searched out that child and called: "Where are you?"

Gen.3:15

Then He broke the monstrous covenant that they had made with the devil with the words: "I will put enmity between you and the woman, and between your seed and her seed."

With that promise He laid the foundation for the restored relationship between Him and ourselves.

In that too He was *holy* and highly exalted in mercy and great power.

Gen.17:7

Later He gave that relationship the form of a covenant. "I will establish My covenant between Me and

10

you and your descendants after you... for an everlasting covenant, to be God to you and to your descendants after you."

Surely we don't think too little of that, do we? Surely we do not take it for granted that God is again our God and the God of our children? For this means nothing less than that the enmity between Him and us has been removed. All is clear again, there are no more barricades.

Ps. 50:7

Put reverently: God could do no more. For He gave Himself: your God am I.

Ex.6:6

In that manner He was again highly exalted. He adopted a people for Himself, His people: "I will take you for My people, and I will be your God..."

Majestic in holiness

Israel was allowed the first hand experience of knowing what it means to have *this* God as their God. When He had brought them out of Egypt, and had led them through the Red Sea, they saw God's holiness:

Ex.15:1&11

> *"I will sing to the LORD,*
> *for He has triumphed gloriously.*
> *Who is like Thee, O LORD,*
> *among the gods?*
> *Who is like Thee, majestic in holiness,*
> *terrible in glorious deeds, doing wonders?"*

Majestic in *holiness*..."that is", according to the Marginal Notes "adorned with exceedingly great holiness". Israel need not think of God's holiness as something remote and of little significance for them. For God's holiness was clearly directed against their enemies, and was terrible in glorious deeds (as in the Red sea and in the Dead sea). And in the pillar of cloud and the pillar of fire, God's holiness was extended protectively over His people who had called to Him for help. And where Israel faced an unsurmountable barrier, there the Holy One of Israel, delivering and liberating, opened for them a highway.

Is.40:25

Centuries later Isaiah could comfort this same people, who were then faced with the wall of exile, and saw no deliverance. And he reminds them that God is *holy.* "To whom then will you compare Me, that I should be like him? says the Holy One." In Him, therefore, Israel may hope again. Isreal never needs to say despondently:

Is.40:27,28,29

My way is hid from the LORD, and my right is disregarded by my God. For He gives power to the faint and to him who has no might,

He increases strength.

He, the *Holy One.*

A strong refuge.

1 Sam.1:15

Thus, in the need of her personal life, which she knew to be closely bound up with the life of God's people, Hannah has known and loved the LORD and poured out her soul before Him. And He heard and answered her prayer.

Then Hannah prayed and said:

1 Sam.2:1,2

> "I rejoice in Thy salvation.
> There is none holy like the LORD,
> there is none besides Thee,
> there is no rock like our God."

He who no longer stands on solid ground, must flee to this rock.

12

Prov.18:10   There is no other. His holy name is a strong tower, the righteous man runs into it and is safe.

Also the poet of Psalm 71, in a long life, has *so* learned to know the LORD:

Ps.71:7   *"I have been as a portent to many;*
but Thou art my strong refuge.
Ps.71:19-22   *Thou who hast done great things,*
O God, who is like Thee?
Thou wilt revive me again."
And his prayer becomes a song of praise:
"I will sing praises to Thee with the lyre,
O Holy One of Israel."

The holy God, He goes with us from our youth to our old age, and beyond. As a strong refuge, a comforter who does great things. Who comforts and revives. Doesn't this fill our heart with joy?

How holy is His name

And God has shown Himself most majestic in holiness when He sealed the covenant once established with the blood of His only begotten Son. For of course we know: God is our God again-that didn't just happen. A river of blood was needed to impress *Heb.9:22*   upon Israel that without the shedding of blood there could be no forgiveness. Therefore the history of Israel draws a trail of blood through the world: child's blood, whenever a little boy was circumcised. Blood of he-goats; blood of bulls; blood of calves; blood, *Heb.10:4*   always asking for something better. "For it is impossible that the blood of bulls and goats should take away sins." Then the *Holy one* of Israel brought this "something better" into the world: His Son, with whom He was well pleased. His blood became the *Matt.26:28*   blood of His covenant, which was poured out for many for the forgiveness of sins.

13

Now, without bloodshed, the water of baptism may sign and seal to us that through baptism we have an eternal covenant with God. An *eternal* covenant. We said this covenant was there at the time of Abraham. It was there at the time of David. It was founded in the blood of David's great Son. It is here today; our children are placed in it. And it will be there in the future: "I will be God to him who conquers, and he shall be My son."

Rev.21:7

That is how holy God's name is. To our redemption.

Mary the mother of the Lord Jesus, sang about this in her song of praise:

Luke 1:50-55

> *"Holy is His name. And His mercy is on those who fear Him from generation to generation.*
> *He has shown strength with His arm.*
> *He has helped His servant Israel, in remembrance of His mercy....*
> *to Abraham and to his posterity for ever."*

The Lord Jesus spoke of it when He prayed for us, who would believe in Him. Then, for our sake, he appealed specifically to God's holiness which protects us and keeps us, as it shielded Israel in the pillars of cloud and fire: "Holy Father, keep them in Thy name."

John 17:11

Is God's holiness only terror, inhibiting our prayer? No, for in His holiness God has opened wide the doors of His heavenly sanctuary:

Ps.50:15

> *"Call upon Me in the day of trouble;*
> *I will deliver you, and you shall glorify Me."*
> He is almighty, for He is holy.

Perfect, for He is holy.

But He is also merciful, for He is holy. He is a refuge and a rock, who does great things for His people. He comforts and revives, for He is holy.

Heb.4:16

"Let us then with confidence draw near to the throne of grace, that we may receive mercy and find grace to help in time of need."

H.C. 120

In childlike reverence, for He is Holy.

In childlike trust, for holy is His name.

4 Along The Stages Of God's Promises

The Bible is no legal contract, an official document which establishes in precise legal wording exactly how matters stand, and that's it. That is not the way it is with God's Word. In it He addresses us, invites us, draws us, encourages us, urges us, commands us, and sometimes threatens us. But He always does so in order to gain our hearts.

Is.65:1

"I said 'Here am I', to a nation that did not call on My name."

Call upon Me.

Israel often understood very little of this. It saw God's covenant of grace as a contract. Psalm 50 speaks about that attitude.

Israel did something: it offered sacrifices.

Now the LORD should do something too: be their God.

Ps.50:18

Meanwhile their hearts were far removed from Him. If they saw a thief, they were his friend, and they kept company with adulterers.

Ps.50:3

Then the LORD comes to His people in fire and tempest.

He reminds them of the old covenant:

Ps.50:7

"I am God, your God."

16

In painful irony He asks:

Ps.50:13

> *"Do I eat the flesh of bulls,*
> *or drink the blood of goats?"*

It is not too much for Him to again vie for the *heart* of His people. He shows them a better way than that where one good turn deserves another.

Ps.50:15A

> *"Call upon Me in the day of trouble."*

For when He himself has once again in His covenant opened the way to His throne, neither for Isreal nor for us is it any longer a question of "take it or leave it". It is not up to us to choose to make use of it, or not. Then He also *commands* that we *follow* that way, not with a harsh command, but with a command unto life, that is suited to us as air is suited to our lungs.

Command and *Prayer* are not opposites: the command is not an iron letter, and prayer is not a spontaneous expression of life. Not at all.

The shell of the *command* hides the pearl of the *promise*:

Ps.50:15B

> *"I will deliver you,*
> *and you shall glorify Me."*

There are no conflicts of interest between God and His people. Our salvation is His glory. His glory is our salvation.

Basic chord

This word of psalm 50 runs like a vein of gold through all the Scriptures. In the Old Testament the prophet Joel prophesied about the day of the LORD.

Joel 2:32

A great and terrible day. The sun shall be turned to darkness and the moon to blood. And who will be delivered?

Joel answers: In Mount Zion and in Jerusalem there shall be those who escape.

Who will escape?

"It shall come to pass that all who *call upon* the name of the LORD shall be delivered."

The words are a little different from those in Psalm 50. They are adjusted to the situation. But they actually say the same:

Ps.50:15

> *"Call upon Me in the day of trouble;*
> *I will deliver you, and you shall glorify Me."*

Acts2:19-21

Centuries later, in the New Testament period, Peter, filled with the Holy Spirit, delivers his sermon to the men of Israel. He, too, speaks of the great and manifest day of the Lord. It will come after blood and fire and vapour of smoke. Then who shall be saved? The answer is that of Joel and of Psalm 50: "It shall be that whoever *calls on* the name of the LORD shall be saved."

And this precious promise, that can give renewed courage time and again to every one who prays, appears for a third time, now in the letter to the Romans.

Here too, in a broader sense, the terror of God's judgment in His great day is dealt with, as is the question of who will be found righteous. Only the Jew? The Greek also?

Rom.10:12,13

Away with those questions! God's gates are open in all directions. "For there is no distinction between Jew and Greek; the same Lord is Lord of all and bestows His riches upon all who *Call upon* Him. For, 'everyone who calls upon the name of the Lord will be saved' ". In every chord of the gospel the basic note of this promise-in-a-command sounds through. It gains admission to God's throne for every sinner. It commands gently: *Call upon Him!*

Is there anyone then who is still justified in saying: Prayer, that is not for me?

Theme and variation.

And yet...

The Lord knows the heart. The fearful heart that is afraid.

The stubborn heart, that is unwilling. The hardened heart, that is unmoved. The sluggish one, that keeps losing Him. That is our heart. And it is not too much for Him to keep on playing the one theme of *Call upon Me* throughout the Scriptures in all kinds of variations and adorned with ever changing motifs.

Is.45:19 N.K.J.V.
"I did not say to the offspring of Jacob,
"Seek me in vain."
He does not let us call Him in vain:

Ps 116:2
"For He inclined His ear to me."
No one needs to think that His voice would fall on deaf ears,

Ps.94:9
"He who planted the ear, does He not hear?
"He who formed the eye, does He not see?"

We could fill page after page with promises as precious as these. We want to mention only one more here, one in which the Lord Jesus Himself gently

Matt.7:7-11
commands and promises: "Ask and it will be given to you; seek, and you will find; knock, and it will be opened to you. For everyone who asks receives, and he who seeks finds, and to him who knocks it will be opened. Or what man is there among you, if his son asks him for bread, will you give him a stone? Or if he asks for a fish, will you give him a serpent? If you then, who are evil, know how to give good gifts to your children, how much more will your Father who is in heaven give good things to those who ask Him."

Therefore *Call upon Him.*

By all means, *Call upon Him!*

Wonderful in His deeds.

Yes, but is that *possible*? How can a *dead* sinner call on God?

Ex.15:11

He cannot. A miracle must first take place. And miracles *do* still happen. For the holy God is working wonders. He brings the dead to life through His gospel.

Canons of Dordt 3&4

By the Holy Spirit He enlightens our mind, so that we will rightly understand the call of His Word. By the working of the same Spirit He also penetrates with His Word into our innermost being. And we become different people. Born anew, born again.

Our ear which was closed, was opened. What is hard in it He softens. He brings our will, which is dead, to life. That which is bad, He turns to good; that which is unwilling, to willingness; and that which is stubborn, to obedience. How that happens we do not know. Supernaturally, mysteriously, inexpressibly. A miracle no less great than the resurrection of the dead

2 Cor.5:17

In greatness it can be compared to a new creation.

Canons of Dort 3&4

Inst.3 20.14

And the first cry of the person reborn is: "O God, have mercy on me, a sinner." Along the stages of God's promises the new man climbs up to God's exalted throne. And *Calls upon* Him. (Calvin)

Confidence

For only in God's promises can we find our confidence. If we have to admit time and again that we cannot stand before God, that even our righteous deeds are like a polluted garment, we nevertheless lay claim to God's gentle command-with-a-promise. And we say: Lord, You Yourself have commanded and promised. *That* is why I *Call upon You.*

And He hears us. For He gladly listens to our prayers. He has assured us of that in the Old - as well as in the New Covenant. He does that with words of promise, and with signs. With the actual gifts of His only begotten Son.

Ex.30:7-10

Lk.1:10

In the Old Covenant, fragrant incense was burnt twice a day on the altar of incense, while the people prayed in the court of the tabernacle.

In the East, when people wanted to honour an important guest, they burnt incense for him. So also the LORD was honoured by the offer of fragrant incense. The people knew that the LORD delights in the fragrance of this sign of honour. For He had after all instituted it Himself. They also knew that, as the smoke of the incense offering rises, so our prayers may rise to the throne of God.

And the LORD gladly heard them.

So Israel learned to approach the LORD with confidence:

Ps.141:1&2

"I call upon Thee, O LORD,
 make haste to me!
 Give ear to my voice when I call to Thee!
 May my prayer be counted as
 incense before Thee
 and the lifting up of my hands as
 an evening sacrifice"

And in the New Covenant?

There we do not find any more symbols. No longer the shadow, but the real thing is found. For now the LORD has given His Mediator. And in His name, which is more than all fragrant incense combined,

Matt.17:5
John 14:13 & 14
we may confidently come to the Father. For the Father loves Him: "This is My beloved Son, with whom I am well pleased; listen to Him!"

Listen to Him when He says: "Whatever you ask in My name, I will do it. . . If you ask anything in My name, I will do it."

John 16:23
Listen to Him, when He assures you: " Truly, truly, I say to you, if you ask anything of the Father, He will give it to you in My name."

Listen to Him, when He opens God's gates to us:
Matt 7:7
"ask, and it will be given to you; seek, and you will find; knock, and it will be opened to you."

For however many promises of God there may be, in Him they find their "yes".

Therefore, because we may go to God by the way of these promises the "Amen" is also through Him, to the glory of God.

Trust

An old man had served the Lord from his youth.

When he was asked what had been the greatest sin in his life, he replied: That I have not *always* put my trust in the Lord.

Trust is the life blood of our fellowship with God, and so also for our prayer life.

Trust means: I am certain that all God's promises are not only for others, but also for me. That the Lord also hears my voice when I cry to Him. That He takes to heart also my pleas which I, in my
Ps.32:8
situation, send up to Him. That His eye is also upon me.

It means that in all my needs and troubles I hold to the certainty of His promises. I know and am assured that the living God is very close to me. In that *trust* I come to Him. For by His mercy, the chasm between Him and me is bridged. Therein the heart of the Holy One of Israel has come to mine. Therein I lose myself in Him. Are my sins so great? So ugly? So hideous and shameful that no other man knows? He *does* know. He already knew before I cried to Him. I cannot and need not and do not wish to hide them from Him. He may search me and know me. They no longer stand between Him and me. For He Himself took them away, when He gave the Lamb of God who takes away the sin of the world. Is it getting dark in my life? Am I surrounded by worries?

Ps.139:23

Ps.71:5

> *"Thou, O LORD, art my hope,*
> *my trust, O LORD, from my youth."*

Saying Amen.

Along the stages of God's promises we have climbed up to the throne of God. We have put our supplication before Him. Then we close our prayers in the name of our Lord Jesus Christ with the word Amen. Our faith, our expectation and our certainty are all expressed in that one word: Amen! What I have prayed, is true and certain. For God has much more certainly heard our prayer than I feel in my heart that I desire this of Him. Our praise and thankfulness are beforehand included in that one word. Therefore we must not use it thoughtlessly.

H.C. 129

We must not use it as *just* a closing word. Our *heart* must say it. Our heart may speak in it - on the basis of God's steadfast promises.

23

5 Is There Any Use In Praying

But why is it actually necessary for us to pray?

Doesn't God know all things? What can we possibly have left to tell Him?

Furthermore, does He not make us do works according to His eternal counsel? Is everything then not predetermined? Can we effect any changes by praying either for or against this counsel?

Living fellowship.

Earlier a word was used with which Satan can give us a hard time: God's *eternal counsel.* God's counsel and our praying, can these co-exist?

Most definitely!

So well, in fact, that in wondering about the use of our praying, we must take our starting point precisely in the counsel of God. For God so counseled with Himself that, in His creation, next to angels, He wanted to create in addition to animals, plants, stars and rocks, also people. Further, He also wanted a living relationship with those *people,* He with them, and they with Him.

Gen.3:8

In the cool of the day the LORD God walked in the garden of Eden with the people.

These were the thoughts of God about us from the

beginning, that He did not want to be without us. And in His counsel He has created us in such a way that we on our part cannot live without Him; we are inclined to Him. Our heart is restless until it rests in God. (St. Augustine.)

Sin has caused distortion. We became enemies of God. That was the end of our walk with God. But God's eternal counsel didn't shipwreck on our sin. For by His Word and Spirit He creates for Himself new covenant partners. And He finds joy again in this, that regenerated sinners come to Him again, live for and before Him again, and speak and pray to Him again.

And through Him the new life in us reaches out to the Living One, as a plant turns towards the sun. Fellowship can prosper again. He wants to be *called upon* as God, Who is and remains Himself - I am Who I am, that is: I am unchangeable, faithful and reliable.

Ex.3:15

Fellowship between God and His people is again possible.

And never again will a fall into sin be able to destroy that what God has restored in Christ: "And I saw a new heaven and a new earth... And I heard a loud voice from the throne saying: 'Behold, the tabernacle of God is among men, and He shall dwell among them, and they shall be His people, and God Himself shall be among them...'" The fellowship and communion with Him shall continue into all eternity.

Rev.21:1,3

According to His *counsel*.

Experience the fellowship

Now we may also experience this fellowship in our life from day to day, in all our doings before the face of God. We may do so specifically also in our prayer.

25

Man is the only creation of flesh and blood capable of speech. That must also become evident. Man must open his heart to his fellow-men. And even more, he must pour out his heart to his Creator and Redeemer. Man is the only creature who is able to talk to Him, and who cannot live without it.

For that reason God gave us the loving command to pray. That fits right in with what He Himself created and re-created in us. It means that He looks forward to our prayer, as the father looked out for the son who was lost.

And if we do not always keep very clearly in mind how essential this fellowship with the Lord is to our life, then He never tires of insisting on it with many promises. For *He* always *does* see how from the beginning He has desired fellowship with His people, and will desire it forever. He does know, and He *always* knows, that according to His counsel, we cannot live without fellowship with Him.

Therefore, on the one hand in our attitude toward *Him* it is this way:

Ps.103:1
> *"Bless the LORD, O my soul;*
> *and all that is within me,*
> *bless His holy name."*

And, on the other hand, towards *us* it is:

Ps.62:8
> *"Pour out your heart before Him."*

Do we want to see both sides in one Scripture verse, the LORD'S side and our side?

Ps.50:23
> *"He who offers a sacrifice of thanksgiving*
> *honours Me;*
> *and to him who orders his way aright.*
> *I shall show the salvation of God."*

In God's *counsel* the one is never in conflict with the other.

His honour is not in conflict with our salvation.

26

The purpose of our praying.

What is the purpose of our prayer?

That we always get our way?

No, it is this, that we have fellowship with the Lord. That we walk with Him, and pour out our heart to Him. He wanted it this way. He was the first in this, and will be the last. For from *Him*, and through *Him*, and to *Him* are all our prayers.

And we, however insignificant we may be, we are a factor not to be neglected in this. Not the toddler in his pyjamas, kneeling by his crib: 'Lord, keep faithful watch over me, also tonight", and not the dying old man, who can now only sigh:

Ps.31:5
> *"Into Thy hand I commit my spirit."*

For God's *counsel* regarding us is such, that He does *not* want to come to His full glory without fellowship with His people. His *counsel* does not make our praying superfluous. It is the only ground of our praying, and that alone makes it possible.

27

6 Not An Information Service

God knows all things. We can never tell Him anything that is new to Him. So praying is superfluous and useless, is it not?

With such reasoning the devil crashes into our lives.

For it is worth a lot to him if only he can keep us from praying. And when the Lord offers us this comfort: All things are known to Me, - then Satan makes his offensive: Then why go on praying?

Keep God informed?

Matt.6:8

It is true: God does not need information from us. "Your Father knows what you need before you ask Him."

Things don't come as a surprise to Him. He never has to say: I did not foresee this. I did not think of that. I couldn't have known about that. He is never at a loss so that He would have to involve us to help Him with our prayers and information. But it is not true that praying is therefore superfluous and useless. For the fact that all things are known to Him before I ask Him opens the way for me to go to Him with more trust . For now I don't, like a manager, need to oversee the course of things in the world, or even only in my own little life, from beginning to end. He does not depend on my report. I do not have to draw His attention to this or that. Fortunately not.

Ps.147:4	*"He gives to the stars their names."* No astronomer need inform Him.
Job 38:28	Happily, He is the father of the rain and begets the drops of dew.
Ps.65:9 *Ps.66:7*	He visits the earth and greatly enriches it. How would I ever know even the tiniest fraction of what is needed for this? And how would I know how to bring it to His attention at the right time? Happily, His eyes keep watch over the nations, also over those whose name I don't even know, let alone that I would be able to lay their needs before Him.
Nah.1:7 *2 Tim.2:19*	Happily He knows those who take refuge in Him, those who are his. And He knows where they live, whether on this side or the other side of the iron curtain. He knows what their needs are, and before I, yes, even before they themselves call to the Lord about them, He will answer.
Ps.139:13	And as far as my personal life is concerned: He has formed my inward parts, He has knit me together in my mother's womb. I do not have to keep Him informed of the processes taking place by day and by night in my spirit and body without my knowledge.
Matt.10:30	But I may trust: even the hairs of my head are all numbered.
Ps.139:16	In His book they were written, every one of them, the days, the good ones and the bad ones, that were formed for me when as yet there were none of them.

So I don't have to put on a front for Him! I don't have to pretend to be bigger or stronger than I am. I *cannot* hide anything from Him, no, nor do I need to. I *cannot* dredge up from the dark shafts of my existence everything that festers and churns there, and it is not necessary for me to do so either. And I do not have to tell Him all that in so many words, in order to be able to stand before Him uprightly.

I can go to Him in a relaxed manner and give myself over to Him:

Ps.139:23-24
> *"Search me, O God, and know my heart!*
> *Try me and know my thoughts!*
> *And see if there be any wicked way in me,*
> *and lead me in the everlasting way!"*

And then I know, that with Him I am in good hands. With all my needs and problems He takes me on - even with those needs of which I myself am not aware.

Give me your heart

We don't tell God anything new.

He does not ask that, either.

Prov.23:26
What He asks for is our *heart*.

Is prayer superfluous, because God knows all things?

Whoever thinks that way does not have a clue as to what prayer means in our walk with the Lord.

1 John 1:5
God is high and in Him there is no darkness at all.

Ps.62:8

Matt.6:8
There is no darkness in the fact that on the one hand He commands us to pour out our *hearts* before Him, and that on the other hand He reveals to our comfort that He knows what we need before we ask Him.

Phil.4:7
In this there is only peace, as He has decreed in His counsel.

7 Is God Inexorable?

But can God be swayed by prayer?

Can He even possibly ever let Himself be swayed by prayer?

In adversity, illness, unemployment?

Has He not from eternity, once and forever made His decisions?

Fixed His plans? These do include everything, don't they, without there ever being a possibility of change? Whether the sun will shine today, where and when and for how long? If I will live to see tomorrow, and how? If there will be peace in a year's time, or war?

Is not God like a programmer who has programmed His computer in such and such a way and that is final? A man like that is no longer involved . He can go home, he can go to sleep, he can even pass away, - the program he wrote will be computed perfectly, also without him.

Did God not do it this way?

Isn't this God's rule: once decided, ever decided? Isn't He chained to His own councel for ever?

Devilish thinking.

The devil greedily uses such thinking. He pounces on us at the most unexpected moments. While

31

reading the Bible, during prayer, during a sermon; on a beautiful holiday, or in the midst of traffic; or, when in deepest misery we are in the greatest need of the trusting relationship with Him. Doubts which have long lain at the bottom of our heart, unvoiced, never quite thought out, suddenly he can throw *Is.46:10* them over us like a net. He even manages to come with Bible texts: "My counsel shall stand, and I will accomplish all my purpose." See, that is what it says!

Jas.1:17 With God there is no variation, or shifting shadow.
N.A.S.B.

And what do you *do* with that?

What God has proclaimed by Isaiah to Israel's comfort; what James could write down to our encouragement, Satan takes this out of context and puts us under the direct fire of twisted words of God. Go on, pray, he sneers, go on, pray against the cliffs of God's unchangeable counsel. They'll all glance off, your prayers. They don't do good to any man.

When someone gets tangled in such snares, it is possible for him to despair.

If nothing can even be changed by prayer, isn't it cruel of God to pacify us with the empty shell of *Call-upon-Me*? Is that fair or merciful? Is that how a father deals with his children? The prayer dies on the lips and in the heart. And small wonder.

Job 38:2 But what have we done? The same thing Job did: we have darkened God's counsel by words without knowledge.

There is only one way.

There is only one way to escape this deadly snare. And this is not the way in which we, like Job, call God to account, and to which the LORD answered at the time:

32

Job 38:4

"Where were you when I laid the foundation of the earth? Tell me if you have understanding!"

Neither is it the way of working it out in our minds.

Is.55:8

God's thoughts are not our thoughts. Our ways, also our ways of thinking, are not His ways.

The only way is that of fleeing to Him.

The way of *Call-upon-Me* in the day of such troubles. Again and again and as often as is necessary.

A foolish way: for how can I flee to that which according to my thinking can offer no refuge?

An illogical way: for how will the strength of my logic be refuted by such a flight?

1 Cor 1:25

Matt.7:24-27

John 7:17

But the foolishness of God is wiser than man, and the weakness of God is stronger than man. If I put my trust in God's promises, then I will find that the house of my life is founded on a rock. If anyone wants to do God's will and walk in God's ways, he shall know of these promises whether they are from God.

Is.63:9

Would the Lord be unconcerned with His decisions once taken, like the programmer with his computer program? If that were true, how then could the Holy Spirit say through Isaiah of the Saviour of Israel that in all their affliction He was afflicted?

Judges 10:16 N.A.S.B.

Is the Lord chained to his own plans? How then is it written of Him that at a certain moment that He could bear the misery of Israel no longer?

We should not try to figure Him out. And then let the result be decisive, whether or not we should *Call upon Him.*

Hos.11:9

For who is like Him, that he would check on God?

Not on a man but on God, the *Holy One* in our midst?

God is God, and we do not understand Him. His counsel shall stand. It is neither rigid nor obscure nor is it a riddle. For He is light and in Him there is no darkness at all.

1 Jn.1:5

He, in His counsel, is not far removed from us. He is always present, in everything that happens to us. And He is always involved, empathizing- with His thoughts, His heart, His decisions. And He is ever ready with His counsel, as often as we *Call upon Him.*

Therefore: flee to Him when you are fearful. For the LORD *does* let Himself be swayed by prayer.

Moses experienced that.

When in addition to showing much unthankfulness Israel also sinned with the golden calf, the LORD made up His mind to destroy Israel. And He told Moses of His decision.

We would say that He could not have been more definite. With this decision the LORD had totally committed Himself.

Ex.32:14

What did Moses do at that point? Did he acquiesce in God's decision, because there was nothing he could do to change it anyway? No, on the basis of God's own promises to Abraham, Isaac and Jacob, he interceded for God's people. And the LORD repented of the evil which He thought to do to His people. God was swayed by prayer. He changed His mind.

And that didn't happen only once. For the LORD took Israel's sin with the golden calf so seriously, that He said to Moses: I will now send an angel along

34

Ex.33:1-3 with you, but I will not go up among you any more, lest I consume you on the way, for you are a stiff-necked people.

And so Moses is faced once again with the wall of decision of God. Pronounced. Declared. Inexorable.

A wall?

Ex.33:13

Ex.33:14,15

But Moses knows the way to God's heart. Again he intercedes- for himself, as the shepherd of the flock. How would he be able to lead them any further? He also intercedes for the people, for what would happen with respect to God's own promises? "Consider too that this nation is Thy people." And what does the LORD say then? Once decided, forever decided? No, but what happens? The heart of the Friend opens itself to the friend: "My presence will go with you, and I will give you rest." And Moses replied: "If Thy presence does not go with us do not lead us up from here."

Then the LORD answers: I will also do this thing.

Moses' prayer did not glance off the cliff of God's decision.

The LORD yielded to his prayer.

Seeing God's glory

How is that possible?

In order to find this out, we must continue to follow the story closely for a while yet to find out.

Ex.33:18

For the fellowship of the LORD with Moses was *so* close, that he asked: I pray Thee, show me Thy glory. And then Moses really sees a glimpse of the goodness of the Holy One of Israel. The LORD reveals Himself to him. For Moses hears a voice proclaim: "The

35

Ex.34:6-7 LORD, the LORD, a God merciful and gracious, slow to anger, and abounding in steadfast love and faithfulness, keeping steadfast love for thousands, forgiving iniquity and transgression and sin, but who will by no means clear the guilty."

Because the LORD is merciful and gracious and abounding in steadfast love, He can yield to prayer. For He is holy.

Num.14:18 In Numbers 14:18 Moses refers to this self-revelation of the LORD. Once again Israel has been rebellious. And again the LORD says: I will destroy them. And again Moses pleads on God's promises. I pray Thee, let the power of the LORD be great as Thou hast promised, saying: 'The LORD is slow to anger, and abounding in steadfast love, forgiving iniquity and transgression."

And then the LORD relents again. For in mercy does He find His glory. Centuries later Joel refers to the same revelation of God's glory to Moses. The day of the LORD is coming, great and very terrible. That is the substance of his preaching.

But does the prophet leave off at the proclamation of an inevitable fate? For what chance is there left now for escape? Surely God's day is coming unavoidably?

Joel 2:12,13,14 But no. Rend your hearts, he calls to Israel. Repent. Who knows, who knows whether God will not turn and repent. "For He is gracious and merciful, slow to anger, and abounding in steadfast love, and repents of evil."

Joel knows that the LORD is not an immovable God who, once He has spoken, will not repent forever, instead, the LORD is a God who can be swayed by prayer.

36

Num.12:13

Thus Moses also prayed for Miriam. She was punished with leprosy. How would she ever recover from that? But then, on the request of Aaron the priest, Moses cried for her to God: "Heal her, O God, I beseech Thee." And the LORD did help her. She became clean again.

Amos 7:1-6

Amos, too, knew that the LORD can be swayed by prayer. He had two visions, one of a coming plague of locusts, and another of a consuming fire. There was nothing mysterious about those visions:

God's judgments were coming, and there is no reprieve.

Then Amos calls out: "O LORD God, forgive, I beseech Thee!"

And then too, the LORD changes His mind. "It shall not be, said the LORD."

God is not inexorable.

Whether I can understand it or not, whether I can reconcile one with the other or not, He has revealed Himself as merciful, gracious and abounding in steadfast love. And that is how I may *Call upon Him* and hope in Him.

8 Praying In Accordance With God's Counsel

James 5:16

"The prayer of a righteous man has great power in its effects."

What kind of power? Conjuring power? Spiritual power pouring out of man?

No. The power does not come from the praying man. It does not lie in the fervour, the earnestness, the faithfulness with which we send up our prayers. The power and the help come from *God*. We ask Him something, as children ask their father. And in response to our asking He *does* something. God comes into action. He helps us to bear our burdens. He removes obstacles and points out ways where we no longer see a way.

Faith can never expect too much.

But it is possible for our expectations to be misdirected. We cannot just ask anything that comes to mind. We cannot wrest from Him all which we have decided to want. God is not inexorable, but He can not be swayed by prayer, as a person's mind can be swayed by convincing talk from someone.

The Holy One in our midst.

God does not hand over control to others, neither His control of the world order, nor of the Church,

38

Hos.11:9

nor of our personal life. He remains *God*, the *Holy One* in our midst.

Num.20:12-13

At Meribah Moses resisted the command of the LORD and did not treat Him as holy. Then the LORD Himself had to sanctify His name before His servant and before His people. "Therefore you shall not bring this assembly into the land which I have given them."

Deut.3:23-25

You cannot but be moved when you read how Moses then nevertheless, besought the LORD to be allowed to take God's congregation into God's land. Had not the LORD revealed Himself especially to him, Moses, as being slow to anger and abounding in steadfast love? "O LORD God, Thou hast only begun to show Thy servant Thy greatness and Thy mighty hand... Let me go over, I pray, and see the good land beyond the Jordan, that goodly hill country, and Lebanon. But the LORD was angry with me on your account, and would not hearken to me: and the LORD said to me, "Let it suffice you; speak no more to Me about this matter." The LORD could not be swayed by prayer. Why not? Because Israel had to learn once and for all to take Him seriously as the *Holy One*. Therefore Meribah left a deep impression. That is why it is again mentioned several times in the Scriptures. See for instance Psalms 81, 95 and 106.

2 Sam.12:14

David had sinned against Uriah and his wife, and had thereby given the enemies of the LORD occasion to blaspheme. After Nathan's rebuke, he confesses his sin. And the LORD took away his sin too. But... the LORD also sanctifies His name. The prophet must announce to the king: The child that is born to you shall die.

39

Does David then acquiesce in this without any further ado? Because it was unchangeable anyway, especially since the child immediately fell ill?

2 Sam.12:22

No. David, too, knew God as merciful, abounding in steadfast love. He fasts, he prays and he spends the nights on the floor. *Perhaps* the LORD would be gracious to him.

But after seven days the child dies. The LORD was not to be swayed by prayer. He sanctified His name before His enemies, His people, and His annointed.

2 Cor.12:7-9

Paul writes that he has been given a thorn in the flesh. A messenger of Satan, who harrassed him. *That* bad!

"Three times I besought the Lord about this, that it should leave me, but He said to me: 'My grace is sufficient for you.'"

God was not to be swayed by prayer. Also in Paul's life He sanctified His name. It was His purpose that His power would only be fully made perfect in weakness, and also to keep Paul from exalting himself too much.

Acts 12

To give *one* more example: Peter had been put in prison by Herod. His sentence was certain: he must die. But earnest prayer was made to God by the church. And the Lord gave help. Peter was miraculously delivered. The Lord is that powerful! But in the same chapter of Acts we read first about James - also an Apostle and a man of the first hour. We would say that, no less than Peter, he also was indispensable for the church. Wouldn't the church have earnestly prayed to God for him? And for Stephen, the deacon of whom we read five chapters earlier that he found death for the sake of his Lord? A man full of faith and of the Holy Spirit, full of grace and power, who did great wonders and signs among the

Acts 6:5&8

people? Of whom so much could still be expected for the upbuilding and growth of the church?

But Stephen and James are *not* delivered. They are put to death. And we are not given any explanation at *their* death.

The Lord went His own, His exalted way.

With Stephen, with James, with Peter, with the young church. He did so as the Holy One in our midst, who does great things for His people, also when we do not understand Him in what He does.

Prayer, hoping for the best?

Do we then pray, hoping for the best? In our prayer, do we throw for the highest prize and then trust to luck and see what happens?

Jer.26:1-3

> *"In the beginning of the reign of Jehoiakim the son of Josiah, king of Judah, this word came from the LORD, 'Thus says the LORD: Stand in the court of the LORD'S house, and speak to all the cities of Judah which come to worship in the house of the LORD, all the words that I command you to speak to them; do not hold back a word. It may be they will listen, and everyone turn from his evil way, that I repent of the evil which I intend to do to them because of their evil doings.' "*

Did Jeremiah have to prophesy, yes, even on the Lord's command, in the hope of a lucky break? Did the LORD send his servant to do this on the basis of the platitude that if it won't do any good, it won't do any harm either? Didn't the LORD know His people? Didn't He know that they were a stiffnecked and rebellious people?

41

He knew this very well.

And *yet* He says: It may be they will listen. It may be they will repent. And then *it may be* that I'll find occasion to repent of the evil which I intend to do to them.

That is how flexible the Lord is in His considerations, how manoeuverable in His ways. There is never an inevitable fate. There is always room for our repentance, and also - it should be added - for our hardening.

Whether we can understand it or not - that is how He reveals Himself and *that* is how He is. Whether we can grasp this with our logic or not - He is *that* free in His decisions and their execution, in which He will work according to the counsel of His will.

And in the same way that He makes the prophets prophesy and so Himself speaks to His people *or* to the heathen - think of Nineveh! - *so* He also teaches *us* to pray - not just trusting to luck, hoping for the best, but on the firm ground of His graciousness, His mercy, and the greatness of His steadfast love. From this, the weary one draws strength. He who has no refuge will flee to Him on that ground. He who sees no way out will go the way of the command with a promise because He commands:

Is.40:29

"*Call upon Me in the day of trouble.*"

Ps.50:15

And that, then, is no gamble.

Prayer on firm grounds.

Israel knew very well that the LORD is merciful. Jonah even had the nerve to reproach Him on the basis of His mercy:

Jonah 4:2

"*Is not this what I said when I was yet in my country? That is why I made haste to*

42

flee to Tarshish; for I knew that Thou art a gracious God and merciful, slow to anger and abounding in steadfast love, and repentest of evil."

But what Jonah threw at the LORD in reproach, Moses took hold of in his pleas for God's people, for Miriam, for himself when he was not allowed to lead God's people into the promised land. It was the firm ground for David and Joel and Amos. It was also the ground for our Lord Jesus Christ when so *Matt.23:27* often he would have gathered the children of Jerusalem who would hear and repent of their evil-doing. It was the firm ground for the congregation of Acts 12. It was also the firm ground for Paul, who had to carry a thorn in his flesh. *This* is how they know Him, as the God who never said to Israel: "Seek me in vain." They know him as the God of Jeremiah 26 who said *it may be* that they will repent. The living God. A bulwark never failing. And that is how they found courage and confidence for their prayers.

Praying in accordance with God's counsel.

To force God to do their will? To push Him away from the way which He knew was best?

No. For they *also* knew Him as the Holy One in their midst, one whose ways were quite often such, that *they* would not have chosen them. They knew him *Ps.23:4* as the good *shepherd* of Psalm 23, who sometimes leads His sheep through the valley of the shadow of death.

Ps.22:5 In Him they trusted, as the fathers had trusted in Him and cried to Him, and were not disappointed.

They knew what it was to leave God to be God, and to let His grace be sufficient for them.

43

This was not their own idea, they had learned by listening to His voice. And we, too, may thus listen to Him. No one does this of his own accord. But that, too, we may ask of Him - that the Holy Spirit from day to day will teach us also through God's Word. In times when we see how He builds His church, but no less when we have to see how He seemingly breaks down and destroys.

Jer.1:10; 45:4

Luke 11:13

And *that* kind of prayer is not fruitless. "If you then, who are evil, know how to give good gifts to your children, how much more will the heavenly Father give the Holy Spirit to those who ask Him."

The Holy Spirit teaches us to pray in faith; we do not pray against God's counsel, nor as if there is no counsel of God. In the way of ongoing prayer He teaches us to heed God's ways and to put our hand on our mouth and to pray according to His will.

What does this latter mean?

That in all things we recognize and firmly believe that He is our Father. Father - that word says it all. When we no longer see a way out, and also when we *do* see the way, but shy away from it because it is so dark and so deep, even then we believe that He is our Father. This means that our prayers, however weak, start pushing towards the completion of God's eternal counsel through the wonderful working of God's Spirit. We do not know this counsel, but we firmly trust that it is always good, and that all things contained in it work together for our good.

H.C.124
Rom.8:28

This means that we do not go to the Lord with *our* designs, with *our* plan, to put that next to or over against God's high plan, in order to push ours through by the strength of our prayer.

The Holy Spirit teaches us by our prayer to pray in a God-fearing manner and to follow Him obediently in our pleas instead of forcing our will on Him in words without knowledge.

We must be obedient as the Lord Jesus was, who learned obedience through His suffering - though without sin - Jesus who in the days of His flesh offered up prayers and supplications, with loud cries and tears, to Him who was able to save Him from death:

Heb.5:7

Matt.26:39

> *"My Father, if it be possible,*
> *let this cup pass from Me;*
> *nevertheless, not as I will,*
> *but as Thou wilt."*

And He was heard for His godly fear.

9 Expectation

We have prayed. We have put our pleas before the Lord. We have said *Amen*:

It is true and certain.

And then?

What do we do next?

Watchtower of hope.

Ps.5:3

"In the morning Thou dost hear my voice, in the morning I will order my prayer to Thee and eagerly watch..."
We pray: before and after meals. What do we expect of those prayers? We pray when we are going to sleep, and when we rise. What do we expect then? We pray at the beginning and at the end of our worship services, meetings, schooldays. What do we expect then? When we pray in troubles, in marriage difficulties, problems in raising our children, in spiritual needs... what are we eagerly watching for then?

For God to hear our prayer? For help? For strength to bear?

Or do we not really expect very much? Do we not take God's promises seriously enough, that we eagerly watch for their fulfilment? And if that is the case, why do we still pray? Out of superstition? Because we do not really dare to drop it? Or because we never know what good might yet come from it?

46

Calvin, with reference to Psalm 5:4 (see above) says that our prayers are sent up into the air in vain if we don't have the living hope in us, out of which we, as if from a watchtower, quietly wait for God. So our prayers are sent up in vain if we only pray to get our way, with the thought that although it might not do any good, it won't hurt either. They are sent up in vain if we see our praying as no more than a psychological self-help method with the idea that a man must after all, express himself once in a while. A man must talk to someone once in a while whether to a psychologist, a doctor, or to a minister. Of course, it does not change the situation, but it can certainly make you feel better. And afterwards you are able to handle things a little better.

But that is not prayer. That is *not* the way God, the Holy One, wants to be addressed.

Ps. 121

When we pray we position ourselves on a watchtower. Then we gaze at the horizon. How long yet? And from whence shall our help come? For we have a living hope that the LORD is coming to help, in answer to our prayer.

James 5:17

Elijah was a person like ourselves. The LORD had clearly told him: I will give rain. The prophet had no doubts about this. He passed on the message to the king that there would again be rain. Did he leave it at that? Did he sit back and wait for things to happen?

No. He started to pray - meekly, humbly, and as a supplicant.

1 Kings 18:42-43

"He bowed himself down upon the earth,
and put his face between his knees."

The stronger and more definite the promise, the greater the expectation: He said to his servant: "Go up now, look toward the sea." And he went up and

47

looked, and said: "There is nothing." And he said "Go again", seven times.

How expectantly do *we* look for the hearing of *our* prayers? If we just fling our desires into the air, we'll never really be *heard*, not *even* if our wishes *are* fulfilled.

Why not?

Because then we do not really receive that fulfilment out of God's hand. Sure, we are in luck. Things are going well for us. But we do not see the *Giver*. That would be impossible.

Ps.123:2 After all, our eyes did not look for Him. Our expectations were not from Him.

I hope in His Word

But what *may* we expect?
All things that we long for? Healing in sickness? Work on periods of unemployment? Children when our marriage remains childless?

Ps.130:5
> *"I wait for the LORD,*
> *my soul waits, and in His Word I hope."*

In His Word!

That means that we may expect what he has *promised*.

And He has promised us a great deal - everything we need to live and die in Him.

But He has not promised us everything we want, nor everything we think we need!

1 John 1:9 He promises us forgiveness of our sins, if we ask Him. We may certainly expect that.

48

Luke 11:13

He promises us the Holy Spirit, if we ask Him. We may certainly expect Him.

John 11:25-26

He promises us eternal life. We may certainly look forward to that. He promises us that He takes care of us, that He is our dwelling place, and that His everlasting arms are beneath us. That was true for Israel and is also true today for God's people. And every member of His people may certainly count on that.

Matt.6:25-34

Ps.46:1

> *"God is our refuge and strength,*
> *a very present help in trouble."*

Every believer may eagerly watch for that, he will not be put to shame- not even when heartfelt *desires* remain unfulfilled.

But we must not raise expectations, in others or in ourselves, which are not grounded in God's Word.

That is what the faith healer does. You can be healed. If only you believe, you will certainly be healed, right at this very moment. The talk-healer takes a word here and there from Scriptures, but he does *not* take the whole of Scriptures into account. He does not read there reverently and carefully how God's ways sometimes can be with His children.

And not only the faith healer, but *all* of us often stumble in our expectations. Who does not eagerly and easily apply words from Scriptures to his particular need? Who does not very easily take one or two passages out of the context of the whole of God's Word, to use those for his particular problems?

Mark 11:24

It *does* say, does it not: . . .whatever you ask in prayer, believe that you have received it and it will be yours?"

Well then!

49

And we sing it, do we not?:
"The hope of faith shall not deceive us."
Well then!

And so we insist that the LORD will make good what He has promised us, meaning that one word, which we took out of the context of the whole Scripture, and wrongly applied to ourselves. And then, if we do not receive what we so ardently desired, if we become disabled, if our husband or wife dies, if one of our children turns his back on the LORD, then we are disappointed.

Lk.22:31 Then Satan shakes us in his sieve, to sift us like wheat. Can we then not trust God's promises after all? And again we mean that one promise that we arrogated to ourselves out of the context of all the Scripture.

Doesn't God hear? And why not?

Doubts begin to rise in our soul.

Haven't we prayed properly? Not truly enough? Not ardently enough? Not often enough? And how truly, how ardently and how often *do* we have to pray then to. . .bend God to our will?

Or: wasn't our faith real? Not strong enough? And how should we then believe to get what we so urgently want to have?

And if the LORD does not re-direct us, does not teach us to see that the cause lies in ourselves and not with Him; that we have not listened to Him attentively and carefully, and thus have not prayed according to His counsel; that we have not waited for Him and not eagerly watched for Him, as we may do according to His Word - then we start seeing Him as a hard master.

1 Kings 18:26-29 We start to see Him as a Baal, to be manipulated by our prayers. Or, we don't see much point in prayer,

50

anymore. Perhaps we do not quite dare to forget about it yet, but we no longer know the waiting in hope and faith.

It is written...

Therefore, when we call to God, we must first listen to Him - and listen *well*, too.

Matt.4:6-7

The devil tempted the Lord Jesus with a text. "If you are the Son of God, throw yourself down; for it is written:

> '*He will give His angels charge of you*,' and
> '*on their hands they will bear you up,*
> *lest you strike your foot against a stone*'".

That is what it said!

But the Lord Jesus did not live by one or two texts. All Scripture was in His heart: "Again it is written, 'You shall not tempt the Lord your God'".

Luke 24:21-32

We must learn to live by the lesson of the men on the road to Emmaus. They also had their own expectations. "We had hoped that He was the one to redeem Israel." But the Lord started with Moses and with *all* the prophets and He interpreted to them in all the Scriptures the things concerning Himself. *Then* their hearts burned within them. We can no longer hear from the mouth of the Lord Jesus Himself what is written in all the Scriptures concerning Himself and His Father, as did the men on the road to Emmaus. But He did send us the Comforter,

Jn.14:26

the Holy Spirit. who will teach us and bring to our rememberance all that He has said to us.

And if someone asks, "How does the Spirit do that" - then the Scriptures have a clear answer. He never

2 Cor.13:14

bypasses the Word of God. Through the Word He comes to us with the grace of the Lord Jesus Christ and the love of God and the fellowship of the Holy

Spirit. And He does not do this as if He has just taken that Word out of nowhere and plunked it on our tables, so that everyone can try and figure it out for himself. No, in His great, and tender concern for us He has entrusted it to His church. There it is

2 Cor.5:20

preached to us by the ambassadors of Christ, the ministers of the Word. There He opens the Scriptures to us, there, in the preaching, in the administration of baptism and the Lord's Supper. He also does so in catechism classes, in the family visits, and visits to the sick, also when those are made by elders or deacons. He does so in the excercise of church discipline. The Lord could have appointed angels for this ministry.

But He chose people, whose ministry is always imperfect. Also, it is only *people* who receive their words in an imperfect manner. And yet there, in the church

1 Tim.3:15
2 Cor.3:8

of the living God is the workplace of the Holy Spirit. There, in the communion of the saints, by teachers to children, through the work of the societies, and in discussions, the Words are passed along, so that our hearts too may burn within us.

Perseverance.

Only when there are well - founded expectations can perseverance in prayer exist.

What is perseverance?

It is not that we have to remind God continually of that which we desire of Him, as if He would ever forget.

Neither is it badgering Him to get this or that done by Him.

Nor is it hammering on the anvil of our wishes with a multitude of words. We should not imagine that the Lord will hear us *because* we persevere so faithfully. If He hears, it is only out of grace, for Christ's sake.

So what is perseverance?

It is this, that we steadfastly expect all things from His mercy and grace.

Ps.103:8
> *"The LORD is merciful and gracious, slow*
> *to anger and abounding in steadfast love."*

These are once again the words with which the LORD revealed Himself to Moses. Through the working of the Holy Spirit we do *not* let ourselves be separated from them. With respect to their contents as well as their frequency and length, our prayers are directed with these words in mind, even when we have to sigh:

Ps.13: 1
> *"How long, O LORD?*
> *Wilt Thou forget me for ever?*
> *How long wilt Thou*
> *hide Thy face from me?"*

Even then we do not let go of Him: instead, through the Holy Spirit, we keep crying to Him, in the certain expectation that He does not deceive us. He does not deceive us in His promise:

Ps.50:15
> *"Call upon Me in the day of trouble;*
> *I will deliver you."*

And he does not deceive in His commands:

1 Tim.2:1-2
> *"First of all, then, I urge that supplications,*
> *prayers, intercessions, and thanksgivings be*
> *made for all men, for kings and all who are*
> *in high positions..."*

For we pray for the church and for the world, for country and people, and for our personal life. But sometimes it does not seem to change anything. Then our faith is being tested. Our walk with the Lord gains depth. And we seek shelter even closer to Him, trusting that we will not be put to shame. Speaking

53

to Him in faith and trust, we keep bringing our needs before Him, pour out our hearts to Him, and ask Him for help. *That* is perseverance.

How long? How often?

Doesn't the Lord become impatient? When we have asked the same thing twice or three times, doesn't He find that enough? He knows by then, does He not? Shouldn't we then just leave it at that? Of course the Lord knows, when we have prayed once. He knew even before we called to Him. Repetition is not necessary for Him. But for *us* it is. For our heart is often disquieted, because our faith is so weak. Besides, Satan never lets up attacking us: Where is *Ps.42:3* your God?

That is why the Lord comes to our aid:
Ps.62:8   *"Trust in Him at all times, O people;*
         pour out your heart before Him;
         God is a refuge for us."
Ps.90:1 That is His honour, to be a refuge and a rock from generation to generation, as often as our heart has need for that. No one appeals to Him in vain.

Luke 11:13 For in answer to our prayer He gives us the Holy Spirit. And then everything is always all right, also when heartfelt desires have to remain unfulfilled.

God is my portion for ever.

And it can happen that desires remain unfulfilled. And it does happen, too, more than once.

2 Cor.12:9 Paul besought the Lord three times that he might be delivered from a thorn in the flesh. Then the Lord let him know that it was all right the way it was and that His grace should be sufficient for Paul. It may happen like that in our life too. A couple may remain childless in spite of many prayers. We may fall ill and grow worse in spite of heartfelt supplications.

Noting God's actions it may then become clear to us that the Lord leads our lives, or the life of someone who is very dear to us, or a matter that very closely concerns us, in a different way than we would like. Then, in our weakness and helplessness, in our loss and deterioration, God's power must be fully revealed. And then that is not an easy way for us. Not at all.

Can we then because we were deceived in our expectations, simply quit praying.

If *that* were true, then how far and how deep did our expectation really go? Was it an expectation concerning only ourself? Or did we, to speak with the Psalmist, wait for the LORD?

Ps.130:5

If He was our first concern in our ardent prayers, then we are not at the end of our expectations when there are unfulfilled desires. Then we need not think: Too bad, my prayer has not been heard - I might as well not have bothered. For then the most profound depth of our expectation comes to light. Then we seek all the more to draw the LORD closer to us, in order that He may indeed show to us His presence and help. Is He not our almighty Father (see also chapter 12 & 13)?

Then the substance of our prayer changes. It more and more becomes a praying - with - the - Lord. A praying - towards- Him, in growing unanimity. Then we seek Him as our portion, and therefore hope in Him. Our soul waits in silence for God alone, because from Him is our salvation. And *so* God's grace is made manifest in our life.

Lam.3:24
Ps.62:2

Ps.73:26

> "*My flesh and my heart may fail,*
> *but God is the rock of my heart*
> *and my portion for ever.*"
And we receive God as an inheritance.

Undoubtedly.

10 A Favourable Answer

God hears prayers. Always?

Does He always answer favourably? Always?

Why do we sometimes seem to be calling on Him in vain?

And what to think then of His promises, promises that just don't seem to be kept?

Those are valid questions, important to us. We should not push them away, as forbidden thoughts. For then they will start acting like time bombs, at a time when we can least handle them. Satan explodes them into our lives, bringing destruction. Don't push them away, but work them out, by the light of the Scriptures.

I do not listen.

Num.14:41
Deut.1:45

Israel went up and fought against the Amorites, contrary to God's express command. They were defeated and wept before the LORD. "But the LORD did not harken to your voice or give ear to you."

Prov.28:9

> *"If one turns away his ear*
> *from hearing the law,*
> *even his prayer is an abomination."*

He who himself does not want to listen to God, should not count on finding God willing to listen to him.

56

When Israel has an altar to idols in every street of Jerusalem, the LORD says through Jeremiah: "I will not listen when they call to Me in the time of their trouble." Even Jeremiah is not allowed to pray for Israel: "As for you, do not pray for this people, or lift up a cry or prayer for them, and do not intercede with Me, for I do not hear you."

Godlessness and prayer cannot go together.

Hindered prayers.

We will have no difficulty with that. After all, with us there is no godlessness, we think.

And yet we should not too easily shrug off the question if our prayers can also be rejected sometimes.

Peter wrote his letters not to the heathen, but to believers.

And what do we read?

"...husbands, live considerately with your wives, bestowing honour on the woman as the weaker sex, since you are joint heirs of the grace of life, in order that your prayers may not be hindered."

The wife must be submissive to her husband. Peter said that very clearly earlier on. But the husband must not misuse this. He may not be a tirant. He must be the head of his wife, in the Lord. And if he is not, who can touch him?

The Lord can touch him then. For He is witness to the covenant between him and his wife. He is always present, also when no outsiders are: In the living room; in the bedroom. If the husband does not honour his wife in the Lord, he may perhaps pray, but his words do not go up before the throne. They are hindered: Something is blocking them.

Would that word be valid for husbands only and not also for wives? Is it valid only within marriage and not outside of it? Is it not valid for all human relationships which are meant to be a blessing and which can be poisoned by the abuse of power?

A common example. In a family the good rule exists that everyone eats what is being served. If need be no more than a single tablespoon. There is spinach on the menu. And little Mary, who is six, does not like spinach. She just cannot swallow it. She is whining beforehand that *she* does not want any spinach.

But that makes father impatient. He serves his daughter a portion. Not *one* spoonful, but three, four big ones. And when little Mary is sick with loathing even before the meal starts, then his look says: No nonsense, eat up, who is the boss here!

And then: pray! Mary too.

And later: give thanks! Mary too.

Prayers that are hindered.

The father's - who was not fair to his child, and so is not right before the Lord.

The mother's - who cannot put her heart into these prayers. For she feels sorry for her child and yet does not want (dare?) to openly contradict the father.

Eph. 6:4

Mary's, and those of her brother and sisters - in their hearts is bitterness, and that is father's fault.

We cannot always enter the heavenly palace, and appear before God's throne any old way. We can not address Him personally in a contrary, angry state of mind.

58

It is just an example taken from plain, ordinary life. We are sinful people. Husbands, fathers, teachers, employers, governing authorities as well as wives, mothers and nurses. Hindrances to our prayer can occur in all kinds of communities. In our families, in our schools, in our meetings, in the church services. We may not go ahead with our prayers and ignore those hindrances. For then the Lord does not listen. But the same letter of Peter, the same chapter, still opens wide the gate to God's palace:

1 Pet.3:12

> *"For the eyes of the Lord are upon the righteous,*
> *and His ears are open to their prayers."*

Who are the righteous ones. No, they are not the good brothers who are quite satisfied with themselves. They are those who do not turn their ears from God's laws but hear them. Who will be taught by them that they are sinners. That they have been made heirs of the *grace* of life. With their wife, with their children, with brothers and sisters. Peter quotes Psalm 34 in this passage. There, it says of those righteous:

Ps.34:17

> *"When the righteous cry for help,*
> *the LORD hears,*
> *and delivers them out of all their troubles."*

Waiting for God's times.

When we humbly *Call upon Him*, God's heart is inclined towards us. He does not stay remote, inactive, but He gets up to help us.

And we watch for that help eagerly.

But we do not always see it coming immediately.

And then what? Do we become impatient? Resentful, when it takes longer than we expected? Does our expectation die down as time goes by?

But have we actually paid attention to God's times?

Is.65:24 The Lord *can* come to our aid very quickly: ". . . Before they call I will answer, while they are yet speaking I will hear."

The servant of Abraham had to go and find a wife for Isaac, a mother for God's people. What a job! Therefore he prayed for God's guidance when he

Gen.24:15 arrived in Mesopotamia. And before he had finished speaking, Rebekah came to the place where he

2 Kings 20: 1-11 was standing. King Hezekiah became very ill: He was going to die. That is what Isaiah came to tell him, on God's command. Then the king prayed. And before the prophet had quite left the palace, the LORD said to him: "Turn back, and say to Hezekiah: I have heard your prayer. . . I will heal you."

And so we could mention many more examples from Scriptures.

Ex.17:8-13 Moses pleaded for Israel when it had to fight with Amalek. And the LORD came to the aid of His people while Moses called and as long as he called. At

1 Sam.7:9 Mizpah Samuel cried for help, and the LORD answered him right away.

Judg.15:18,19 At Ramath-lehi, when Samson was in danger of dying of thirst, he cried for God's help. And God split open the rock and water came out of it, so that he could drink, and his power returned and he revived.

But it can also be different.

Jer.42:7 Jeremiah prayed for the defeated remnant of Israel that was without a shepherd. It took ten days before the LORD answered him.

Dan.10:13 Daniel fasted and prayed for his people. It was twenty one days before he received an answer. Did the LORD not care about His people and His servant during all those days? Is that why it took Him so long to take action? No, but there was strong opposition. The angel Michael had to come and help overcome it.

And these were only matters of days.

Gen.12:4 Abraham was seventy five years old when he left Haran. God gave him His promise: He would become a great nation.

Gen.21:5 He was one hundred years old when Isaac was born. In between lay twenty five long years of waiting and hoping against hope. For he saw that his body and Sarah's womb were past begetting and bearing a child. Twenty five years...

Only then God's time had come.

Isaac and Rebekah bore the same promise of Abraham.

Gen.25:20,26 They remained childless for twenty years before the LORD gave them Jacob and Esau.

Israel was cruelly oppressed in Egypt. They had to drown their small sons, the hope of the people. They lamented about their taskmasters. And those living by the promises given to Abraham, Isaac and Jacob, how they must have cried to the LORD, but nothing changed.

Did the LORD not hear; did He not see; had He forgotten His promises?

Ps.10:1 *"Why dost Thou stand afar off, O LORD?*
Why dost Thou hide Thyself
in times of trouble?"

And who could know that the LORD was already on His way to help His people?

Already with the birth of Moses?

Ex.2:9-10	When he was raised, for the first few years of his life, by God's promises in his father's house?
Acts 7:22	When for years he was instructed in all the wisdom of the Egyptians, and became mighty in words and deeds?
Heb.11:25	When he chose rather ill-treatment with the people of God than to enjoy the fleeting pleasures of sin?
Ex.2:14 & *Acts 7:27*	When Israel rejected him with the words: "Who made you ruler and judge over us?"

When he gained forty years of experience in the desert?

Who *could* have known it?

But after that it became visable: God's time had now come.

<table>
<tr><td>Ex.3:7-8</td><td>He had most certainly seen the misery of His people.</td></tr>
</table>

He knew their afflictions.

Therefore he came at *that* time to deliver them.

By then, however, eighty long years had passed.

Another example:

<table>
<tr><td>2 Kings 11</td><td>Athaliah, a daughter of the heathen king Ahab, destroyed all the royal family in Jerusalem. In one fell swoop the house of David became a branchless trunk. How the believers of that day must have moaned to God.</td></tr>
</table>

Would God's promises to David and his house be unfulfilled?

The years passed. And no one could know that the LORD had indeed remembered His promises from the beginning. That a one year old toddler, a son of David, who was hidden in a bedchamber, was being brought up in the fear of the LORD.

Only after six years that little boy was proclaimed king.

Only then it became clear: the LORD had not forgotten His promises after all.

And do we ever think of the believers who lived after the last prophet had spoken his last word? This word: "Behold, I will send you Elijah the prophet before the great and terrible day of the LORD comes. And he will turn the hearts of the fathers to their children and the hearts of the children to their fathers, lest I come and smite the land with a curse." Where was this comfort of Israel? Generations came and went. What did they see? A poor and oppressed people, bowed down under the yoke of the heathen. They could rightly say, as in the days of the exile:

Ps.74:9
> *"We do not see our signs;*
> *there is no longer any prophet,*
> *and there is none among us*
> *who knows how long."*

It was more than four hundred years before the Saviour, Christ, the Lord, was born.

God's times can seem endlessly long.

And we want to mention one more example.

Rev.6:9-11
John saw under the altar the souls of those who had been slain for the Word of God. He heard them cry out: "O Sovereign Lord, holy and true, how long before Thou wilt judge and avenge our blood?" And they were told to rest a little longer: Till God's time would come. Meanwhile nineteen centuries have past...

God's times

How would *we* have reacted if we had had to call for seven, twenty five, eighty, four hundred years

Ex.17:7

before the Lord came? Would we not have asked: Is the LORD with us, or not? Would we not have complained: We call upon Him in vain?

2 Pet.3:4

Where is the promise of His coming? Is it only mockers, who ask that? Or does also our own heart sometimes think in that direction? How eager is our expectation for that "little while" to be over? And to

Rev.6:11

come a little closer to everyday life: We pray for the needs of church and country and world. For the future of our children and grandchildren. Surely, these are no small affairs! But is there really much change as a result of our pleas?

Ps.55:22
1 Pet.5:7

And as far as our personal life is concerned: we cast all our anxieties on the LORD. We may do that, He says so Himself. But how much do we really notice at times that He cares for us? When we fall ill, when we are unemployed, or when we become old, or when we face death? And then if the Lord does help, in His good time, do we actually still notice? Do we see then that the Lord has heard after all? Do we see that though He tested us, not one of His words has been untrue?

Or was our hopeful expectation not durable enough to watch for such a long time, and to wait for God's times?

Heeding God's ways.

A faithful old shoemaker told how poor he and his family had been. They were so poor, he said, that sometimes there was no money in the house to buy bread. He said that sometimes he had thought that now there is only one way left in which the Lord can help us: By putting a purse of money by the door. But, he continued, He always sent someone with a

64

pair of shoes that needed mending. When I had repaired those, money again came into the house.

So simply, in such an ordinary way the Lord can come to help in our needs. Do we pay attention to that? Or do we have a ready-made solution in the back of our minds? A purse of money, for instance, to be put by the door? And do we therefore neglect to notice God's hand when he comes to our aid in a different and ordinary way?

We sometimes look to the east, thinking that our help must come from there. And then, if it comes from the west, do we still see the hand of the Lord in it?

We are unemployed. We call on the Lord about this matter. Of course, we also apply for jobs. Sooner or later we are called for an interview! Of course we do the best we can. And. . .we are chosen out of ten or more applicants!

How happy we are! But do we see in this very ordinary chain of events the hearing of our prayers? Or. . . do we think about how we have really watched for that job very eagerly and about how we have managed very nicely?

Or we have become seriously ill. We are taken to the hospital and we are examined. We hear that we have to face a serious operation. Our prayers go up to God: Father, grant us that we may live!

Then we are wheeled into the operating room. All the knowledge and expertise of modern surgery and nursing are brought into play. And. . .the operation is successful. We may recover and go home again. We may sit down again in the accustomed place, *Ps.30:3* amongst loved ones and surrounded by familar things once again. We cried to God and He has healed us. Are our hearts and mouths then full of that? Or do we talk to every visitor about the man in the

65

surgeon's coat? And can't we say anything more profound than: "It's amazing what they can do these days!"

When we live close to the word of the LORD, we do not see any luck or chance. Then we see Him in His goodness over us.

Ps.107:43 *"Whoever is wise,*
let him give heed to these things;
let man consider the steadfast love
of the LORD."

What the Psalmist speaks of does not come naturally. We cannot do that of ourselves. But also for this we may call on Him, that He will teach us by His Word and Spirit. Then we see: it is really true, the LORD hears, He answers. Many of His children have experienced this more than once. They experience it daily, in big things, in little things, in family problems, in difficulties at work, in the relationships with colleagues, with pupils, with supervisors, with subordinates, in the church, in hopeless situations, and when facing a difficult discussion.

This is not just pious talk with no substance. It is truth. We can depend on it and look forward to it. Everyone who wants to serve the Lord will experience it.

We must remember, however that the Lord is omnipotent. He helps and gives deliverance in His good time. He comes in His own way. And that is quite often in the way of an old pair of shoes.

Unanswered prayers

Do we then always receive from the Lord what we ask for? Health when we are ill, work when we are unemployed? Children when we are childless?

66

Certainly not?

Well, are some prayers of righteous people then unanswered?

Not that, either. After all, if that were true how could we close all our prayers with *"amen"*?

1 Jn.5:14
But there is a great difference between *unfulfilled wishes* and unanswered prayers. In our wishes we are shortsighted and sometimes even sinful. But by God's grace we learn to submit our wishes to the Lord's will. Would we ever want to use Him to push our ideas, against His will? Would one want to continue living, against His will? Would one want to cling to his wife, to his child, or to his business, when knowing that the Lord wants differently? Who would dare to do that? Where would our faith be then? Would we then have surrendered to Him? And where would the honour of God be?

Matt.26:37

Lk.22:44
In Gethsemane the Lord Jesus saw before Him the hellish agony He had to suffer. That certainly did not leave Him unmoved, for He was truly man. He became sorrowful and afraid. His sweat became like drops of blood. Then He prayed: "My Father... let this cup pass from Me..." Was this a sinful prayer? Was it disobedience? Did our Saviour go against the Father in this?

No, but He did shrink with abhorence from the dark road He had to travel. This was because of the inclination created into human nature, to flee away from its own destruction, so it says in the Marginal Notes on Matt. 26:39. But He did submit in everything to God's will: "If it be possible..." It was *not* possible. Out of love for us, the Father had decided otherwise. Was the prayer of the Son then unanswered?

True, the inclination of His human nature to escape

67

the hellish agony was not fulfilled. But His prayer, in which He had submitted His nature to the will of God, was most definitely heard: "He offered up prayers and supplications, with loud cries and tears, to Him who was able to save Him from death, and He was heard for His godly fear..." And when He had finished all, the Father raised Him from the dead. That was answer to prayer!

Heb.5:7

We, too, may see a road before us which according to our human nature we would avoid at any cost. We may be threatened with the loss of a husband, wife, or child; blindness, dementia, depression may be looming over us. Father, Father, let this cup pass from us!

And we also contend with the fact that we are short-sighted, sinful people who do not fathom God's ways. We can hardly even believe that He sees further and knows better than we do. Therefore the not-my-will-but-Thy-will passes our lips only reluctantly. And we have such trouble recognizing the *hearing* of prayer when our wishes are *unfulfilled*.

And we have not even mentioned James' admonition:

Jm.4:3

> *"You ask and do not receive,*
> *because you ask wrongly,*
> *to spend it on your passions."*

This is to have crossed completely the boundary of what is right and fitting. After all, if we are only and solely concerned with ourselves... May we then in our troubles not come to God with our heartfelt wishes? We may always do that. How else could we live for Him? But coming to Him in the name of Christ, means among other things, that we submit our desires to the law of Christ, the same law to which He submitted His human nature, the law of Thy will-be-done, in which we put all things into the hands of our Father who is in heaven. Then our

H.C. 129

prayer will always be true and certain. For it is much more certainly heard of God than we feel in our heart that we desire this of Him. Therefore we can always say *amen.*

11   Reading Carefully

2 Pet.1:

"First of all you must understand this, that no prophecy of Scripture is a matter of one's own interpretation, because no prophecy ever came by the impulse of man, but men moved by the Holy Spirit spoke from God..."

The prophets have never put their own pious thoughts on paper. The Holy Spirit moved them. The Bible is not a word of man, but the Word of God.

How then could we be allowed to use that Word in any way we please, to break the unity of Scripture by picking out certain promises, without carefully reading them, and without considering their context and the whole of Scripture?

That is what it says, doesn't it?

A young man had been ill for years. He wanted so very much to be healed. He fervently prayed for this to the LORD because is He not almighty? And does it not say in Mark:

Mk.11:23,24

"Truly I say to you, whoever says to this mountain, 'Be taken up and cast into the sea', and does not doubt in his heart, but believes that what he says will come to pass, it will be done for him. Therefore I tell you, whatever you ask in prayer, believe that you have received it, and it will be yours."?

That is what it said! Do not doubt...Believe that it will come to pass...Believe that you have already received it. So he really had to put his *faith* to work. On *that* would depend whether or not he would get better. It was a despairing, disappointing struggle in the loneliness of his sick-bed.

How many people have similarly struggled with certain promises? How many people have prayed and have been disappointed? Often it is through ignorance. Sometimes it is because young people have not yet gained experience in using the Scriptures. Sometimes, after years of health problems, after they have tried all and sundry different cures and remedies, people finally turn to a faith healer. And promises like the one in Mark 11 turned into whips, driving them on. The blind man had to believe that he could see again, the deaf man that he could hear again. If only they truly believed it, it would certainly happen. And so it was a foregone conclussion: If they were not healed, it was perfectly clear that they had no faith and no part in God's promises!

And so people have come into crisis.

Was this because promises are unreliable?

No, but because they have not been read carefully and in the context of the whole of Scripture.

"That is what it says, is it not?" they thought. But there is one thing that they did not understand: - that no prophecy of Scripture is a matter of one's own interpretation and that each passage of Scripture must always be read and understood in the context of the doctrine of the whole Scripture. And so they actually did not know what it really said.

71

Perhaps there are still people struggling like that, even today. To help them we will read a few of those powerful promises which can be easily misunderstood.

Stunts with trees and mountains?

What is Mark 11 all about, the text from which the sick young man picked out a promise? About our wishes and about how these can be fulfilled? No! What did happen here? The Lord Jesus had cursed a fig tree. Why? Because He found no fruit on it.

Wasn't that a strange thing for the Lord to do? Could the tree help it? Does the Lord Jesus fight against trees? Is that the task of our Saviour? No, that is not the way to approach this miracle. What then is the way?

Jer.19:10,11

At the end of His life on earth the Lord Jesus was in a position of humiliation. For three years He had struggled for the heart of Israel. But the people and their leaders did not want themselves to be saved. They did not bring forth fruits of repentence. Then the Lord gave a sign. That was nothing extraordinary. The prophets before Him often had done the same thing. To give one example: Jeremiah was told by the LORD to go and buy an earthenware jar. He was to take along some of the elders of the people and go to the Potsherd Gate. The *Potsherd* Gate. The name already indicates what could be found nearby - a sort of a refuse dump.

> *"Then you shall break the jar in the sight of the men who go with you and shall say this to them, 'Thus says the LORD of hosts: So will I break this people and this city, as one breaks a potter's vessel, so that it can never be mended'..."*

72

A clear sign, one which the people understood very well.

And so now our highest Prophet also gives a sign. He curses the tree that bears no fruit. And the curse has become fact. Already on the next day, the disciples see it. "Rabbi, look! The fig tree which you cursed has withered."

Mk.11:21

They understand perfectly what the sign meant: just as this tree died so will it be with Israel and its leaders, with the high priests and the scribes, whom they, as ordinary men, looked up to. But how would that be possible?

At the time the disciples did not yet know what is awaiting them. They do not know what role they will have to fulfill once the Lord has been taken up from the earth. They do not know that in only a few months' time, this curse over Israel is to come true, through their preaching. But the Lord does know. And now already He comes to help their unbelief: Have faith in God. In *God*. Have faith, not in the strength of your own pity, not in the power of your weak human words, but in *God*! For *He* will do it. *He* fulfills His work of salvation of which Moses, the Psalms, and the Prophets spoke. More than once God's salvation came in incomprehensible and seemingly dead-ended ways. So it was in the house of bondage, Egypt, in the Red Sea, in the desert, in the exile, in the stump of Jesse. And now, now in Christ this salvation has come very close. And He, the Son of the living God, will make it advance by withering the tree of Israel's existence. For that will mean no less than the reconciliation of the world.

Is.11:1

Rom.11:15

And to him who is like the disciples, who is called to serve in this work of salvation it can be said that, if for that reason he would say to this mountain, "be taken up and cast into the sea", and does not doubt

73

in his heart, but believes that what he says will come to pass, it will be done for him.

That is strong language. Does that give us license to play stunts with trees and mountains to get the whole world to follow us with wonder? No, the meaning is that through this teaching, the disciples, may now already learn that power is from *God*, and that their words and work will be irresistable as long and as often as they speak and act in the Lord.

Rev.13:3

Later the Holy Spirit will remind also them of these words of the Lord. He will do this when Stephen is stoned, and when James is killed by the sword, when Peter is in prison, and when Paul is a prisoner for years, when Trophimus has to be left ill at Miletus, and when Timothy turns out to be not strong physically, when John is exiled to Patmos. And these things will be *after* the garden of Gethsemane, where the Lord *Himself* will pray to the Father, where He in His heart will not doubt but believe that what He prays for, will come to pass. If ever there was anyone who could have had his wishes fulfilled, it was He.

Tim.4:20
Tim.5:23

"Do you think that I cannot appeal to my Father, and He will at once send Me more than twelve legions of angels?" He was not bluffing! He could have if He had wanted to, but He submitted His will to the will of the Father: "How then should the Scriptures be fulfilled, that it must be so?"

Matt.26:53

Matt.26:54

Therefore: "Father... not as I will but as Thou wilt."

Matt.26:39

Therefore: "Peter... put your sword back into its place..."

Matt.26:52

Therefore His good confession before the Sanhedrin and before Pontius Pilate.

Matt.26:64
1 Tim.6:13

Therefore He does not come down from the cross when the high priest together with scribes and elders taunt Him to do so.

The Spirit of Pentecost brings all this to their remembrance. When they are immediately faced with the mountain of the Sanhedrin and its threats, than it happens that Peter and John in turn bring the curse of the fig tree closer by saying "Whether it is right in the sight of God to listen to you rather than to God, you must judge. . ." Then when they are released they pray with the others, without doubting: "And now, Lord, look upon their threats, and grant to Thy servants to speak Thy Word with all boldness. . .while signs and wonders are performed through the name of Thy holy servant, Jesus." And when they had prayed, the place in which they were gathered together was shaken; and they were all filled with the Holy Spirit. That is how mountains were moved into the sea.

Acts 4:19

Acts 4:29,30

Acts 4:31

Mk.11:23,24

Mark 11:23 & 24 is not about our affairs, however important they may be in our life. It is about the great cause of God's work, and it is about the important place our prayer may have in that work. That is what the Lord promises us here. In *that* work He is with us, "always, to the close of the age." For Matthew 28:20 - from which these last words are taken - deals with the same great work of God. In prosperity and in adversity, our personal life and our way of life may also be subservient to that work. Sub-servient: that is quite different from having the things of our life put into our hands in order to bend them to our will through the power of *our* prayer. Faith lives by promises. And it takes note of these promises very carefully, and not arbitrarily.

Matt.28:20

We will leave it at that.

75

It will be given to you.

Matt.7:7
There is another promise which we must read carefully, without arbitrarily drawing it to ourselves. When the Lord Jesus assures us: "Ask, and it will be given you," - what will be given to us?

All we heartily desire? All we honestly think we can not do without?

In Matthew 5, 6 and 7, the Sermon on the Mount, the Lord Jesus teaches His disciples that they are the salt of the earth, the light of the world. That is quite something. It means to keep all the commandments: do not kill, do not commit adultery, if necessary pull out your eyes or cut off your hand; keep your oaths; do not take revenge, love your enemies, do not seek the praise of men; put the Father central in your prayer; expect your salvation from Him alone; do not be anxious, do not judge. It sure is a narrow gate through which we must enter into life. And who is able and willing to do so?

Then the Lord Jesus shows the disciples - and us - the way of prayer. Via that way the Father will give us all we ask of Him, to enable us to be His disciples.
Matt.7:11
Verse 11 says He will give us good things, and Luke 11:13 says He will give us the Holy Spirit.

All this we will receive if we ask Him. And then it is always good, also when heartfelt desires must remain unfulfilled. For then we receive Him as our portion, our eternal inheritance.

76

In My name.

Jn.15:16

"I chose you and appointed you that you should go and bear fruit and that your fruit should abide; so that whatever you ask the Father in My name, He may give it to you."
We may come before God's throne in the name of God's own beloved Son. It is as if that Son were standing there Himself, as if He who sent us was saying: "Just go, don't hesitate to go in My name."

Isn't that powerful? Doesn't that give support and confidence? Does this not mean that we can force things to go our way? Does this not mean that the Father is really obliged to do what is needed according to our honest view?

But what is that to pray in the name of the Lord Jesus?

Jn.13:13

It is to pray on the only foundation of His work of reconciliation, but then in such a way that our prayers are, as it were, filtered by His will. It is to pray along His lines, as He Himself prayed. We call Him Teacher and Lord, and we are right, for He is that. And if then *He*, in His prayers kept the commands of His Father, then we too ought to keep them in our praying. For His prayer and ours must not clash before God's throne.

Matt.26:39

And we know *how* He prayed. In Gethsemane he prayed: if it be possible...

Matt.26:54

Not as I will, but as Thou wilt...and here there were not twelve legions of angels.

After all: "how then should the Scriptures be fulfilled?"

Jn.14,15,16

But what do we do with this text of John 15? After all, it *does* say ...whatever you ask the Father in My

77

name, He may give it to you. See also chapter 14:13; 15:7; 16:23-26. Yes, but what does it say here? What is John 15 all about? It is about the true vine, the Lord Jesus, and about the vinedresser, the Father. It is also about branches, that is, the disciples and us. It speaks of how those branches must bear fruit.

For this bearing of fruit, the Lord has chosen and appointed first of all, His disciples, but he has appointed us as well. And whatever is *needed* for that, we may ask of the Father in Jesus' name. Then He will give it to us in His time and perhaps in another way than we think best. But is He not the wise vinedresser who prunes the branches? Does He not do so by His Word, by His Spirit, and sometimes by way of handicaps, illness, and mourning? We must than accept this pruning, in submission to Him. In the name of His dear Son, we pray to be allowed in that name to bear fruit for Him.

I will deliver you.

"Call upon Me in the day of trouble;
I will deliver you, and you shall glorify Me."
Once again we listen to the words of this Psalm.

Doesn't it say very clearly that Israel under the Old Covenant would always find deliverance from all trouble when calling on Him, both as people, but also as individual members of that people?

Could Israel not manage to get things her own way?

Couldn't every God-fearing Israelite make his wishes known to God to have them fulfilled?

Gen.27:1

But what about Isaac who was blinded for years?

Gen.35:19-20

And what about Jacob who lost his young wife?

And the little boys of Israel who were drowned in the river Nile?

Ex.1:22   And their parents?

Lev.21:17-21   And what about the descendants of Aaron the priest who had a defect and therefore were not allowed to serve in the tabernacle or temple? What a tremendous grief for each faithful priest's son who had a defect, to whom God gave these stipulations, but whose defects He did not take away!

Ex.22:22-24   And what about the widows and the orphans and their dead husbands and father, concerning whom the LORD gave laws in advance?

Lev.13&14   And the lepers in Israel?

Lev.19:14   And the deaf who must not be cursed; and the blind before whom one must not put a stumbling block?

Num.27&36   And Zelophehad, who had no son to whom he could leave his inheritance?

1 Sam.4:19-22   And the wife of Phinehas, who died with the birth of her son?

1 Sam.22:18-19   And Ahimelech the priest and eighty five priests with him, and all the inhabitants of the city of priests, Nob: men, women, children, and babies, who were put to the sword?

1 Sam.31:2   And Jonathan, the ally of David, who fell slain on Mount Gilboa?

2 Sam.4:4   And Jonathan's son Mephibosheth, who had to go through life as a cripple from that day on?

2 Sam.2:16   And the twelve servants of David who fell together in their zeal for David?

2 Sam.2:23   And Asahel, who died in his fight for David?

1 Kings 21   And Naboth?

2 Kings 4:1	And the widow of one of the sons of the prophets, and her god fearing husband?
2 Chron.24:20-22 *Lk.11:51*	And Zachariah, who was stoned to death between the altar and the sanctuary, such an injustice that it is later mentioned by the Lord Jesus?
Esth.2:7	And Esther's parents, who had to leave their daughter behind? And the poet of Psalm 88.
Ps.88:3	*"For my soul is full of trouble,* *and my life draws near to Sheol."?*
Lk.2:37,38	And Anna who was a widow for so many years?
Heb.11:37-38	And all those of God's children under the Old Covenant who were stoned, suffered mocking and scourging, who were sawn in two, killed with the sword; who went about in skins of sheep and goats, destitute, afflicted, ill treated, wandering over deserts and mountains, and in dens and caves of the earth?

Did the believing Israelite not know these things? Did he not see them?

He knew them all right. He saw them daily before his eyes. Sometimes he even struggled with them, with blindness, handicap, death, persecution, injustice. . .Who can say how often he might have called on the LORD in those situations?

What was he to do with the promise of Psalm 50? Was it not spoken by the LORD Himself? Could He not be held to His promise? Yes, certainly. But the believing Israelite *also* knew that the LORD had not given the helm into the hands of His people and into the hands of every individual Israelite. For His people He remained the LORD, God, holy in their midst. They also knew Him as the God of Psalm 22, who could be so far from helping them, so far from

Ps.22:1-2 the words of their groaning. They knew Him also as one to whom they could cry by day and by night without an answer.

Didn't that shake Israel's faith?

No, for God's people do not make God's words and deeds a simple matter of arithmetic: by which they compare what is promised with what has often been done contrary to expectations and so arrive at a percentage of reliability.

No:

Ps.22:4-5
> *"In Thee our fathers trusted;*
> *They trusted and Thou didst deliver them.*
> *To Thee they cried and were saved;*
> *in Thee they trusted and were not*
> *disappointed."*

Those words are in the same Psalm 22.

Israel continued to *Call upon Him*. It continued to hope in His Word.

Matt.27:46 The Lord Jesus hoped in the same word of the same 22nd Psalm when He was forsaken by God. And today God's people still hope and have their expectation in that same word.

Do they do this to better themselves? No, they do it to bring thanksgiving as a sacrifice to the Lord.

And:
Ps.50:23
> *"He who brings thanksgiving as his sacrifice*
> *honours Me;*
> *to him who orders his way aright.*
> *I will show the salvation of God!"*

The salvation of God.

The good.

The Holy Spirit.

81

As an inheritance.

Suffer mocking.

We may not tear any words out of the context of the whole of Scripture, so that armed with these in so-called faith, we might go after illness, unemployment.

Would we wish to have others do that with our own words, taken out of context? Of course not. Well, then it is an unholy business to go ahead and do it with the Words of God. We have to handle these words carefully and reverently in faith.

And that results in mockery of us by the world. The world then says, "What earthly use, what good is praying to you?"

And it results in mocking also by others, people who with Bible in hand really say nothing but the same thing. These people travel highways or byways with their spiritual zeal, and say to us: There is no faith among you. For you don't take God at His Word. *They* have faith, they say.

In mass-meetings they urge on the searching souls with the whip of arbitrarily interpreted promises. And they are successful too. Many people become confused and mixed up. They scorn and mock the church of Christ, where, according to them, everything is dull and lifeless, and where, according to them, the people do not live by God's promises.

We can bear this mockery can't we? And we do not get confused, do we? A straw-fire burns out quickly, but the fire of the Spirit keeps on burning, the fire of the Spirit, who takes *all* of God's Words and puts into our minds *all* that Christ has taught us.

12 The Fruit Of Prayer

We do not pray to better ourselves by it. But we *may* expect our prayer to have results.

Phil.4:6-7

> *"Have no anxiety about anything, but in everything by prayer and supplication with thanksgiving let your requests be made known to God. And the peace of God, which passes all understanding, will keep your hearts and minds in Christ Jesus."*

The *peace of God*, that is the fruit of our prayer promised by the Lord. We may expect to receive this peace without a shadow of doubt.

The peace of God.

What is it, *that peace of God?*

It is not that our wishes are always and immediately fulfilled. Neither is it an unfounded feeling that the Lord will make sure that everything happens the way we want it to. Sometimes people even call that *trust!*

Gen.1:31

Peace in the Bible means that everything is good, whole and in order, functioning well. There was peace in paradise, first of all between the LORD God and the people, and therefore, also between Adam and Eve, and between man and the rest of creation. God saw everything that He had made, and behold, it was very good!

Is.54:10   This peace *we* have destroyed. But in the *covenant* of peace the LORD has restored it. In that covenant the LORD imparts peace again:

Num.6:24-26   "*The LORD bless you and keep you:*
The LORD make His face to
  shine upon you,
and be gracious to you;
The LORD lift up His countenance
  upon you,
and give you peace."

Num.6:27   So the priest had to bless God's people. And it was not a powerless wish of a kind, devout man. No: "So shall they put My name upon the people of Israel, and I will bless them."

The LORD God was behind this blessing.

Eph.2:14-16   In the Lord Jesus Christ this covenant of peace has been confirmed, in His blood. He Himself is now our peace. Therefore God's peace can be laid upon *us* also in every church service:

1 Cor.1:3   "*Grace to you and peace from God our*
Father and our Lord Jesus Christ."

That is not a powerless wish of a well meaning minister either. No: in this way by means of His servant, the LORD puts His covenant of *peace* upon us. And He Himself stands behind it.

All is right again between Him and us. This peace permeates our life as a merciful warmth, for now we know ourselves to be in the right place again - with Him. Now we also know and experience that He accepts us with all our needs and difficulties. Now we can rest in Him again, assured in Him, just as it was once in paradise. Now we know that the Lord can make ways where we no longer see a way, and we live out of His hand from moment to moment. That is the *peace of God.* And it has been definitely promised to us.

Passes all understanding.

That peace is beyond all understanding.

We try to get our heartfelt wishes fulfilled with the help of our mind. We arrange, we take care, we make plans. And when we have everything arranged to perfection, we are satisfied. And that is all right. You even *must* do that. Our mind is a gift of God and we must definitely use it to take care for the future. Scripture teaches us that.

Prov.6:6
> *"Go to the ant, O sluggerd;*
> *consider her ways and be wise."*

1 Tim.5:8
And if anyone does not provide for his household, Scripture says that he is worse than an unbeliever.

But our mind is finite, and, besides, it is darkened by sin. It, therefore, often falls short. We cannot gain a perspective on all things, let alone foresee them or see part of them. Things, therefore, often turn out differently than we had thought. And the peace we had acquired, thanks to having used our mind, becomes a little shaky. In that peace we can never be quite *serene.*

Ps.147:5
But the LORD is great, and His understanding is beyond measure. With Him things do not get out of hand. He never needs to say: I could not have foreseen this; I did not think of that; I could not prevent that. Therefore His peace is beyond any peace our mind can ever bring about.

In His peace we rest completely.

85

Kept by the peace of God.

Phil.4:6

That is why verse 6 of Philippians 4 can start with the words:

"Have no anxiety about anything."

Being anxious really means to have an incomplete trust in God. It means not daring to put things into His hands, not daring to leave them with Him, not really knowing them to be safe with Him. Being anxious is wanting to direct and control things ourselves.

Lev.26:36

No one is able to do that. And what are the results? We become fearful, worried and restless. We look at the circumstances. We are tossed to and fro. The sound of a driven leaf can put us to flight. We lack the sense of peace of God, for we have not lived by what He has made known to us about *our* own unstable mind, and our high-mindedness in His Word.

Prov.16:9

"A man's mind plans his way,
but the LORD directs his steps."
Our mind cannot bring about a lasting peace in us.

Only the peace of God is lasting.

It keeps control of our heart and our thoughts:

Our heart - that is our innermost self.

Our thoughts - that is everything that goes on in our mind.

Heb.6:19

Those are kept, and protected, so that our thinking doesn't wildly take off any which way. Fearful ideas invading our mind do not pursue us. Our heart has its sure and steadfast anchor. As a military command keeps a firm hold of a position, so we are kept safe and protected. The enemy without cannot take hold of us. And within us there is no dejection, but firm confidence. Thanks be to Jesus Christ, our Lord, who Himself is our *peace*.

Do we no longer have any desires?

Would we not dearly love to have those fulfilled - the healing of husband, wife, child, or of ourself, the removal of stress, of grief, of loneliness?

Certainly. Certainly.

Rom.8:20 & 28 We can be intensely happy before God, but also intensely sad. Yet we are kept in His *peace*, knowing in our heart that He makes all things work to our good. We are assured that nothing can separate us from the love of God, which is in Christ Jesus, our Lord, who is the *peace* of our peace.

We do not pray to better ourselves by it.

Ps.73:28 But it *does* make us better. For being kept in the peace of God is beneficial for body and soul and spirit.

He who is kept by God, is kept well.

Christian idealism.

Do we always experience these things that way? Does this give us support in all circumstances?

Who can wholeheartly answer that with "yes"

But that really is how it should be, some people think. They have an idea of how a Christian ought to be, an ideal they keep before them and by which they measure themselves and others. A Christian must always be quietly confident. Thus that is what he indeed is. He must always be happy. And *so* he is always happy, always radiant with joy. "Praise the Lord" is always on the tip of his tongue. For in this way he thinks he is a living witness of Christ.

Weaker sheep of the Good Shepherd are easily impressed and pressured by this. For, alas, *they* are not always happy, they are not always jubilant. Their face does not always radiate thankfulness. And so they feel themselves to be poor witnesses of their Saviour.

Their Saviour? The danger is great that they will be pushed away from Him, and that the devil will not leave them alone.

Do you have no joy, he will ask? Do you then really have faith?

Are you not quiet in the Lord? Was there then real prayer?

Is everything well between Him and you? Or are you not quite sure? Perhaps *that* is the reason why God's peace cannot fill your heart?

Yes, if God does not prevent Satan, he may go even further. He may ask:Why can't you seem to find the peace of God? Where is your God?

Ps.42:4 Is He really there?

A dark chasm can open before your feet.

The image of the ideal Christian is an idol, an idol *which* does not keep our heart and mind in Jesus Christ.

Only the *peace of God* does that.

How

But how does that happen?

Many a heart yearns for peace and certainty, but remains restless. We can reach out to it as a thirsty man

88

reaches for water. How, how can we share in that peace?

What is the answer? The peace does not happen without our involvement. The peace of God does not just come to us. It comes into our life by the way of Phil.4:6, the way of prayer and supplication with thanksgiving.

Phil.4:6   Have no anxiety about anything.

Let your requests be made known to God.

Our requests...That does not mean anything that comes into our head. They are those things which we have thought about very well, which we desire strongly, and for which our heart yearns.

In *all* things.

Does anyone know of anything that is not included in this?

Matt.6:25-34   Whatever occurs in our life, great or small, important or insignificant, we may reverently put it before the Lord. Anxieties about life, food, drink, clothing? He knows that we need these things. Troubles in marriage, raising the children, difficulties on the job? Perhaps unemployment? We may personally address Him about those issues. Are there difficult decisions to be made? Have we put in an important job application? Are we facing an exam or a test, or an assignment? Do we stand before the everyday problems of everyday things in the everyday household? Then we may enter into His high place with these things and place them before Him. And so draw the Lord nearer to us, that He may indeed show us His presence and help.

As sensible people.

Let us not turn ourselves off but be involved. Let us be involved with our mind, our own capabilities and those of other people. There are such strange ideas about living out of God's hand. For instance, should you consult a doctor and use medication when you are ill? Isn't that proof of unbelief? Should we not discard the mind and human help? In the desert Israel was guided by no less than the LORD. In a pillar of cloud and of fire He went before His people. Can any better guidance be imagined?

Heb.3:2
Num.10:29-31

Ex.3:1

And yet Moses, who was faithful in God's house, says to Hobab, his brother-in-law: "Come with us. . . for you know how to encamp in the wilderness, and you will serve as eyes for us." Moses wanted a leader, a guide. After all, hadn't he kept the flock of his father-in-law for forty years? But *under* the pillar of cloud he is glad to make use of the experience of a born and bred desert-dweller.

It is a sad thing when, for religious ideals, people refuse to see a doctor when they are ill. That too is a kind of ideal of being a true Christian. This ideal is a hard master.

And it is so sad, because it denies God's mercy. The teaching of God's Word is neglected. As if He, who came to the aid of His people by means of the knowledge of Hobab, would forbid us to make use of the knowledge and expertise of a doctor. The LORD does not ask from us that we *stop* using our mind and the means available. He asks that we do not use these means in *unbelief*. He teaches us that, for instance, in the message about Hobab, who was not even an Israelite. In our work, in illness, in trouble we may and must do what we can. And as far as the

90

result is concerned, we must prayerfully expect all things from Him, in supplication, with thanksgiving.

Flesh and blood Christians.

In that way are we kept - not as idealists trying to find peace in some train of thought, but as flesh and blood Christians, who can fall ill, who can suffer hunger and can be sorrowful, and who can become afraid and bowed down:

Ps.88:15

"...I suffer Thy terrors;
I am helpless."

Matt.26:37-38

All that is not sin or a falling from God's hand. In Gethsemane the Lord Jesus Himself was sorrowful and troubled even to death.

Out of His fear He cried to God with tears.

No one needs to feel guilty about his tears.

Ps.73:26

No one needs to force joy into his face, while his flesh and heart fail. The Lord is not so in-human that He would ask that of His children. On the contrary:

Prov.25:20

"He who sings songs to a heavy heart
is like one who takes off a garment on a
cold day
and like vinegar on a wound."

That is a word of God. That is how He teaches us according to our human nature. There is a place in our life for sorrow, in which, however, God's peace yet keeps us.

Ps.103:14
Heb.4:15

When God made *peace* with us in Jesus Christ, He knew our frame very well. He remembered that we are dust. He, therefore, has given us a high priest who is able to sympathize with our weakness, a high priest who in every respect has been tempted as we are. The house of the peace of God is not a house of slavery. We are not being pushed in that direction. No one has to live above his spiritual station. It can happen

91

that because in business, family or health things are not quite going our way, that we sinful people become discontent.

I Jn.1:8
Can.of D. 5.1

Can.of D. 6
Rebellion deep in our heart is not impossible. We are not strangers to any sin, not even when we have been regenerated by the Spirit of God. Those times of rebellion are dark and dangerous for a child of God. But God, in His mercy, does not completely withdraw His Holy Spirit from us at such times. He does not leave us to ourselves, to turn our backs on Him for good. He causes us to seek our refuge yet again in our only Mediator, our peacemaker. And the dissatisfaction and rebellion in us because of trouble, change into dissatisfaction with ourselves. They change into displeasure and loathing of ourselves because we trusted so little in Him. That is the way in which the peace of God so powerfully keeps us.

Step by step.

On this way we walk our whole life long, step by step. On it we learn how the Lord can deal with us. Both young people, and old people, in prosperity, in adversity, in life's gains and in life's losses, we gain experience, also experience in prayer. Can the peace of God then not lift us up above all difficulties-in such a way that we ourselves and others will be amazed?

Yes, that is possible and often does happen, even when sorrow overwhelms us. In a mutilated life, and at the graveside of a husband, wife, or child, God's faithfulness can be praised with a praise that passes all understanding. So powerfully does the *peace* of God keep us in such times.

But after that we must go on with the sorrow, the emptiness, the loneliness, the invalidity heavy in our life, year after year. Then the praise may well turn into silence, and even into being mute. But even *then* the keeping by the *peace* of God remains, in a different way, yes, but not in a lesser way, or less powerfully. For on such a long road, such a heavy road we, who are kept powerfully in the *peace* of God, still do not turn away from the Lord. And whoever knows his own sinful, straying heart, he knows that, *that* too, passes all understanding.

> *"Here knowledge stops,*
> *and learnedness goes under,*
> *The wise man wanders past,*
> *the thinker shakes his head,*
> *There is no other way,*
> *God's peace will work the wonder,*
> *He who believes is blessed."*

(G. Waanders, My Confession)

13   A Blessing For
Ourselves

The first cry of a person newly born in the Spirit
is a prayer for mercy. But that is not all. The Lord
does not create new life to further leave it to its own
devices. The wonder continues to work. *He* works
it out. He continually works in the new man. He so
moves and strengthens his will that, like a good tree,
it may be able to produce the fruit of good works,
also of prayer.

How?

Growth and fruit.

Inst.4;1.1
2 Cor.5:18-19

Calvin has beautifully expressed this ongoing work
of God in an example. To those to whom God is
Father, he says, the church must also be a mother.
For the ministry of the gospel, the ministry of reconciliation has been entrusted to the church.
Through it we learn to know God's Word, His promises. And because God is not a man, that He should
lie, we learn to know God Himself through the
ministry of the church. So the church is like a mother
bearing children to her husband, a mother who then
takes care of those children and brings them up. And
she does this in the church family. The Lord did not
place us in the world as isolated individuals, as one
separate person here, another separate person there.
He took us into His family with other brothers and
sisters. There we have communion together as the

communion of saints. We have this communion first of all below the pulpit, where the bread of life is administered to the whole family. We also have it among each other. We may be a hand and a foot to each other. We need not do any pioneering on our own.

Within this communion parents may and must instruct their children in God's Word. In the schools and catechism classes this instruction continues.

In the communion of saints we speak together about the things God has given us, also about our prayer life. We speak to each other in societies, when we are visiting, as boyfriends and girlfriends, as engaged couples, as married couples. Or we read about these things of God in the Bible, a book, or a magazine. Also in that way the Lord works in us. It is true that our personal prayer life is a delicate matter. We do not advertise it to the world, nor should we do this. Perhaps that is one of the reasons that we tend to speak about it rather too sporadically. But prayer can also become a difficult thing. We can get confused and go into a wrong direction with it. We can foster unhealthy expectations and are then perplexed about the outcome of our prayers.

Ps.25:8,9   Then the LORD will turn us back to His paths - for He Himself will lead us, - but as a rule He does that in the way He Himself has provided for: in the way of instruction by our mother, the church; by the communion of saints. And he does not do this without our involvement: we must *seek* His instruction. He does not do this in a flash of magic either, but, yes, he does it wonderously and powerfully.

For He helps us through the preaching.

Besides that, and as a follow-up, it may be necessary to talk with others, also about difficulties in our prayer life, if we have those. It may be necessary to talk with our minister, our elder, or with husband or wife, friend or girlfriend, father or mother. Reading also may help us.

Eph.4:15-16 *"Speaking the truth in love, we are to grow up in every way into Him who is the head, into Christ, from whom the whole body that is the congregation, the church - is fitly join- ed and knit together by every joint with which it is supplied."*
When each part is working properly, this creates bodily growth and the body builds itself up in love."

We grow, and that builds up the body. For in the final analysis even in our personal prayers *we* ourselves are not most important. We are not in any way in- volved in personality development. In us everything concerns the church, the temple of the living God.

Members of one body

As members of the same body we have much in com- mon. We are all sinners. We all must live by grace alone. We all have the daily struggle against sin. What happens in the church, the nation, the world - it con- cerns us all.

So there will also be much which we have in com- mon in our personal prayers.

But we cannot leave it at that.

For we are each one of us different people with our own nature and peculiarities, as well as our own sins and our own circumstances. Within this one com- munion of saints there are healthy and sick people. There are people with a well-shaped, sometimes beautiful body, and others who are handicapped or blemished all their life. They are rich and poor, young and old, married and single, happily married and those with marital difficulties, happy parents and childless couples, people who always prosper, and others who always have problems, people with a good job, and people who are unemployed, people who are mourning, lonely, oppressed.

Prov.14:10

"The heart knows its own bitterness,
and no stranger shares its joy."

These words also apply to *nature, character,* and *disposition.* One has an optimistic disposition, an other is pessimistic. One is spiritually strong, the other weak. Next to the well-balanced personality in the congregation lives the nervous, unstable one, next to the active figure, the more passive one. You'll find the sharp-witted thinker as well as the simple soul, the heterosexual and the homosexual.

And how the lives of God's children are mishapen by their *sins!*

They are warped by greed, avarice, ambition, and lust for power. Some have to fight against the sins of gossip and slander, others against the sins of lying, pride, egotism, intemperance, addiction, contention, laziness, and bossiness.

Often we are not aware of how we are. Sometimes we'd rather not know it either. Where our sins are concerned, who wants to admit to himself to be narrow-minded, jealous, a busy-body? To be impure in mind, or even in speaking and acting? There may be areas in our lives that we leave tightly closed. Where the need of evil festers. Others do not know about it. We ourselves do not want to think about it.

And where our nature and disposition are concerned: Who will easily admit to having a difficult nature? To being a waverer? Not at all the tough guy everybody takes him for? Not the strong-willed man who is not to be upset by anything or anyone? Who will admit that he is often out to appear the cool guy in the eyes of others?

We act the part, put on a mask. That may fool others, - but not the Lord.

And as far as our *circumstances* are concerned: who has always a clear insight into those? Who is willing to accept them? To admit that it bothers him that a promotion to which he felt entitled, did not come through? That it does not sit well with him that his status did not end up being what he had hoped? We keep up a front of being big, and brave, and tough. We do not discuss it with anyone. We push it out of our thoughts and out of our prayers. But it gnaws at the root of our lives.

How will the miracle of rebirth in the Holy Spirit be able to work through in such people?

Stand in the sunshine of God's righteousness.

Solely and only by God's mercy.

But then we must go and seek that too. And draw it to ourselves. If you want to enjoy the sun, you must go and stand in the sunshine. So in our prayers we must put our personal life in the light of God's countenance. Admit Him into our life: His words; His promises, His powers.

Rev.3:20

He stands at the door and He knocks. If anyone hears His voice and opens the door, He will come into him and eat with him, and he with Him.

Admit Him, not because He would know about our *nature*, our sins, and our *circumstances*. We really are not telling Him anything He did not know. We cannot keep even the smallest thing hidden from Him. In *that* we see the miracle of regeneration in action: for us there is no longer any need to hide things either. We would no longer want to, even if it where possible. On the contrary: we want to open the doors of our life and bid Him enter.

98

He *does* know all about us:

Ps.139:1
> *"O LORD, Thou hast searched me*
> *and known me."*

And as for us, we desire nothing more than that He will know all about us.

Ps.139:23-24
> *"Search me, O God, and know my heart!*
> *Try me and know my thoughts!"*

So our prayers are not confined to generalities. They become really *personal* prayers with personal content. For, our will at first being refractory, now moves toward God. The flower turns toward the light. Does that really make a difference? If God's Spirit searches all the hidden places of my heart anyway, does anything really change when I myself admit Him into it?

Can.of D. 3 & 4.2

Does anything change?

Everything changes!

The LORD really knows everything about David's sin. And yet David says:

Ps.32:3-7
> *"When I declared not my sin,*
> *my body wasted away*
> *through my groaning all day long.*
> *For day and night Thy hand was*
> *heavy upon me;*
> *my strength was dried up*
> *as by the heat of the summer."*

But when he started to talk--when he placed himself before the throne of God and laid open his life before God, then everything changed:

> *"I acknowledged my sin to Thee,*
> *and I did not hide my iniquity;*
> *I said: 'I will confess my transgressions*
> *to the LORD';*
> *then Thou didst forgive*
> *the guilt of my sin...*
> *Thou art a hiding place for me...."*

Beneficial

Has there ever been something in your life that nobody knew about - a disease, a sin, a difficulty, or whatever? Something you struggled and struggled with, and you couldn't work it out? You thought you were the only one who had to cope with such a problem. Until you could stand it no longer, and talked about it with someone else. Perhaps hesitantly, afraid of being missunderstood. And then... you heard that the other person knew it too, the same need, the same depression. He knew all about it.

Do you remember what a liberating experience that was? You were no longer alone, no longer an exception. When we in our prayers acknowledge to the Lord what bothers us, we experience something similar. When we tell Him what is ugly in us, mean, dirty, insurmountable, irreparable damaged. What *peace* we find in that. For Him, we do not have to keep up appearances. With Him we can be ourselves, totally, we may pour out our heart to Him.

But not only that. And not that in the first place.

For what help would it be to us if all we could do is talk about things and for the rest everything would remain the same? But He is also the only One who can really help us, and who also *wants* to. Who can forgive us, heal us, deliver us.

Calling on Him, every believer may open the doors and windows of his life to the sun of God's righteousness. God's righteousness, that is His faithfulness. You can depend on Him, he will do what He has promised. *For* us, but also *in* us; in our personal life. What is the result of this new life in us?

First of all this, that we no longer stand alone. The Lord has taken charge of us with all our needs, and keeps doing that from day to day. And further: that through Him, by His power, we put on the new man, who is created after the likeness of God in true righteousness and holiness.

Because we are doing so well in our prayers, so knowledgeably, so psychologically justified?

No, but because the Lord shows mercy to those who pray, and frees them from bonds, breaks through walls, and gives deliverance. That is benefical, that is medication. It is the miracle of life from death.

Once again: we do not pray to better ourselves by it. But we *do* indeed get better from it, healthier. For

Eph.5:8 while once we were darkness, we now are light in the Lord. And we start walking as children of light.

God's hand reaches far

Perhaps someone will say: yes, that may all be well and true for some people. But I do not have that much insight; not into *myself*; not into my *sins*; not into my circumstances. There are days when in the evening I am not aware of having committed any sins. And do I really have to become some sort of a do-it-yourself psychologist in order to be able to pray personally?

Thankfully not. For not we ourselves do expertly, thoroughly know our innermost. A miracle was needed to make us into new men; the same supernatural power is also necessary to make us *live* like new men. It is time to say that self-knowledge does not just happen to us in this new life; that the Lord engages our own active faith. But on the other hand it is no less true that an unspiritual man, however well-qualified he may be as a psychologist, sociologist, or even theologian, does not receive the gifts of the Spirit of God. For they are folly to him, and he is

101

not able to understand them because they are spiritually discerned. In daily regeneration also in the try-me-and-see-if-there-be-any-wicked-way-in-me, it is true that knowledge ceases and worldy wisdom goes under. That God's merciful grace alone works the miracle, he does not understand.

For what I cannot do of myself, He can do. What I do not see in myself, He does see. What I do not realize about myself, He knows. also the unfathomable depths of my subconsciousness. His hand reaches far. Farther than my farthest reaching thoughts. He knows my circumstances, my sitting down and my standing up, my going and my lying down. He is familar with all my ways. He knows my sins and my sinful nature. He does not only try the minds and hearts, He also knits them together. My frame was not hidden from Him while I was still in my mother's womb; not my consciousness, not my subconscious.

Ps.7:10

Ps.139

He knows from far my thoughts, my vague desires.

Ps.90:8

My secret sins He places in the light of His countenance.

Ps.25:8-9

And if we lack insight, we may humbly ask Him for it. Whatever is necessary to gain we may then expect it from Him. It may be by way of a sermon or through a discussion or by reading books? *He* will lead us step by step. For He Himself has awakened in us the plea of Psalm 139:
"Search me, O God, and know my heart."

So through our mouth God calls to God Himself. And would He then not hear? Would he not answer?

David had not studied psychology. But through the Spirit he wrote Psalm 139 and 32 and 51. Many simple children of God did not even know the word psychology. But they opened their hearts to the Lord, to the teaching of His Word. And their lives were healed, in powerful, supernatural renewal from day to day.

From day to day

Yes, for if we do live by the power of the supernatural, we do not live by the attention-drawing spectacle.

Lk.5:8
Gal.2:11-14

Certainly, God's Spirit can open our eyes to sin and perdition in a flash. Peter said: "Depart from me, for I am a sinful man, O Lord." Yet, years later he too needed a reprimand, an enlightening word. And he received that in the simple way of the communion of saints, from an apostle who came to the Lord even later than he.

So the Lord can suddenly illuminate a part of our life. As if a curtain were drawn aside, things may come to light which we had never taken notice of before. In such a way that from *that* moment on we start to repent from a sin. But then we also discover how unyielding our heart really is, and how tenacious the root of sin. How we cannot shed our past like an old garment. A wrong way of thinking can keep its hold on our life from our youth on. How much effort and how much working of the Holy Spirit is needed then to cut away from that? From the idea of ideal-Christianity, for instance. From the doctrine that a man must continuously examine himself to see if he may really belong, to determine if the marks of regeneration and repentance are to be found in him. How has someone heard speak about God's church, from his childhood on? About the offices in the church? About the ministry of the Lord? At home, in catechism classes, in the sermons, in discussions?

Unscriptural forming can leave a dark trail in life. How has one's education been about God's covenant of grace? And about baptism? How do we live by our baptism? *Do* we live by it? Do we teach our children what it means to be baptized? Damage once done, can actively affect a life for years. Certainly, one single sermon can cut through bonds. One single talk can bring new light of discovery. That *is* possible. But usually then too the teaching of God's Word will be needed for a very long time and from day to day, to straighten out what had grown crooked.

And who doesn't daily need the teaching of Scripture? For how easily do we drift away from that which we knew to be good! Think of king Solomon: he started off so well, and yet, when he was old, his heart was no longer wholly true to the LORD, his God. From day to day God's Spirit wants to guide us by God's Word. Wants to open our eyes to things which we had never looked at before. From the depths of our being He brings things to the surface which we never, or not very clearly, were aware of before. Enmity against God, evil thoughts, fornication, theft, murder, adultery, coveting, wickedness, deceit, licentiousness, envy, slander, pride, foolishness. We detest ourselves more and more. By the Spirit we flee the more often and the more humbly to our Redeemer. We cleave to Him whose blood was poured out for the complete forgiveness of all our sins.

1 Kings 11:4

Mk.7:21,22

Form for the Lord's Supper

An eternal covenant with God

And then we never need to give up hope. We don't have to think that we are a lost cause anyway. Not when in weakness we fall into (the same) sin, either. We do not need to doubt God's grace, nor remain in sin. But then we may remember that we have an

Form for Baptism

104

Ps.51:13 &
Can. of D. 5.6

Jn.2:25

Rom.8:29-20

eternal covenant with God. That He will not take His Holy Spirit from us. For even if we disappoint ourselves, we do not disappoint the LORD. He knows what is in man. The triune God, Father, Son, and Holy Spirit, knew who we were and how we were when He decided to work His good pleasure in us all. He did not say: I had better not start on this, it is a hopeless task anyway. He did start on it. And He daily continues in it. Those whom He foreknew, He also predestined, to be conformed to the image of his Son, in order that He might be the first-born among many brethren, and those whom He predestined He also called; and those whom He called He also justified: and those whom He justified, He also glorified. We have been delivered from the bondage of sin. Freed from the burden of our guilt. God lifts our head on high, and we will wear the crown of glory.

How?

As proud people who have overcome sin? As praying experts, who know exactly how to assess ourselves and to make it quite clear to the Lord what their shortcomings were?

Rom.7:21

No way! Daily we experience it: when I want to do right, evil lies close at hand. We are not finished when we have taken this sin or that problem before God's throne once. The proud man does not only accept illness, trouble, difficultites, sin, old age, but also joy and blessings from God's hand.

H.C.:116

But it is *that* hand that reaches far, passing our understanding. That works in us the miracle of life through the Holy Spirit, if we ask Him for this constantly, day by day.

Form for
Baptism

Till we shall finally be presented without blemish among the assembly of God's elect in life eternal.

14 A Blessing For Others

Our personal life is interwoven with that of others. The Lord wanted us to live in relationships with family, friends, colleagues, with church, country, and society. Therefore our prayer can never be just a tête-à-tête between God and the soul. It always stands in the midst of time: God's time; right in the world.

God's hand reaches farther

1 Pet.3:9

God's hand reaches far in our personal life. But it reaches even further - to the end of the earth. The Lord has delivered us that we might be a blessing in this world.

That is why in the Old Testament we often read of intercessory prayers and intercessors.

Gen.18:16 ff

Abraham interceded for Sodom, appealing to God's justice.

Gen.20:7

He also prayed for Abimelech, that he might live.

Ex.8;9;10

Moses offered many intercessory prayers, e.g. for Pharaoh, and for Miriam.

Num.12:13
Ps.106:23

More than once he stood in the breach for God's people, appealing to God's covenant, God's promises, God's mercy.

Ex.32:11-14
Num.14:13-19;
16:22

Samuel, David, Solomon, Hezekiah, Isaiah, Jeremiah, Amos, Ezekiel, Ezra, Nehemiah, they all put a wall of prayers around God's people.

106

Deut.9:25-29	The situation is the same in the New Testament. The
Lk.22:32	Lord Jesus says to Peter: "I have prayed for you that your faith may not fail."
Jn.17:9	He prayed for those who are His: "I am praying for those whom Thou hast given Me."
Jn.17:20	"I do not pray for these only, but also for those who believe in Me through their word."
Rom.8:34 *NASB*	He still prays for us: "Christ Jesus is He who died, yes, rather who was raised, who is at the right hand of God, who also intercedes for us."
1 Jn.2:1	"If anyone does sin, we have an Advocate with the Father, Jesus Christ the righteous."
Matt.5:44 *Lk.23:34* *Acts 7:60*	He commands us to pray for our persecutors. He Himself did so for the soldiers who crucified Him. Stephen did so for the Jews who stoned him.
2 Cor.13:9	Paul prays for the Corinthians, the Philippians, the Colossians, the Thessalonians.
3 Jn. 2	John prays for the beloved Gaius.
1 Tim.2:1	The churches are urged to pray for the apostles and their work. and for all men, while kings and all who are in high positions are especially mentioned.
1 Pet.3:9	When in the inner room we send up our personal prayers, indeed, we close the door, but we do not shut out the world. We do not shut out our neighbour. We bring our personal needs before the Lord, but no less the needs of others. For we have been called to bless, also in the continuing work of prayer, that we ourselves may also obtain a blessing.

The reach of the intercessory prayer

Jam.5:16	*"The prayer of a righteous man has great power in its effect."*

Jam.1:1	Thus writes James, the servant of God and of the Lord Christ.
Jam.5:17-18	James points to Elijah, who was a man of a nature like ourselves. He prayed fervently that it might not rain, and for three years and six months it did not rain on the earth. Then he prayed again, and the heaven gave rain, and the earth brought forth its fruit. Do we believe that? In times of trouble, in sorrow, in problems, do we then act accordingly? When there are problems somewhere, or sorrow, we quite readily say: I will pray for you. But how faithfully do we do that? And how often do we really enter into the heavenly palace like Elijah did and talk to the Father about that matter in the name of the Lord Jesus?

Around the year 200 Tertullian, who lived from 160 to probably well after the year 220, wrote a little book about prayer. It is the oldest known writing about this subject. In it he speaks, among other things, about the reach of prayer, and says that it can "strengthen the weak, heal the sick, cleanse those who are possessed, open prison doors, loosen the shackles of the innocent. Furthermore, it blots out sin, it drives back temptations, it halts persecutions, comforts the faint-hearted, strengthens the high-minded, accompanies those who travel far, and calms the waves; it perplexes robbers, feeds the poor, guides the rich, raises the fallen, steadies the unstable, gives support to those who stand."

Do we realize this? Or do we actually do more talking than pleading? Do we criticise others more than we pray for them? Do we really call on the Lord in *all* needs?

That counts for all of us, for young people, but also for older ones.

The average age in our century is higher than in any other previous one. So there are many aged people; people with lots of spare time. Does that also mean that there are more intercessors?

People with an interest in others, who spend time on others, and pray for them?

In the paper we read about all kinds of needs. We hear about them on the radio, and perhaps see them on t.v..

What do we do about these needs? What do we do *for* them? Is our intercessory prayer in time with them? With earthquakes, floods, revolutions, famines, concentration camps? With increasing crime, errosion of authority, violent and revolutionary strikes? With high-level conferences?

There are many lonely people these days. They feel cut-off. They sometimes wonder: Why am I still alive? What is left for me to do?

What can they do; they, people like Elijah! They can fold their hands, enter into the heavenly palace. Go before God's throne. And speak to Him, yes to Him, personally, about the needs of all christendom, all humanity, all creation.

Pray for...

What needs?

The Lord Himself will show the way to whoever prayerfully asks himself that question. We cannot prescribe programmes for each other. World days of prayer with world wide prayer subjects by which we, world-wide, storm the heavens - those we do not need. While mentioning one thing, we'll fail to mention another. Nevertheless let's give some direction to our thinking.

We may pray for family members, relatives, friends, neighbours, colleagues.

We may pray for the lonely, the sick, the handicapped, and for their relatives and those who take care of them.

Rev.1:12,20 We may pray for the church of Christ, that it may be a lampstand and may spread light. For office bearers and members of the congregation.

We may pray for the preaching, catechism classes, home visits, and visits to the sick. For meetings of consistories, classes, synods, for the education and teachers of preachers, for the unity of the church, for foreign and persecuted churches, for erring churches and straying believers. We may pray for persecuted Christians, when they are slighted, when it is made difficult for them to raise their children, we may pray for them in imprisonment and death.

We may pray for the mission work, for all the work done on the home front, for the missionaries and all their needs, for heathen people, who have become brothers and sisters in Christ and who now must confess His name in their world; We may pray for the young congregation and their office bearers, for those on the mission fields who teach in the name of Christ at schools, give instruction in matters of health and hygiene, who give medical care, and carry out technical services.

We may pray for the work of evangelization.

We may pray for couples who are expecting a child, for parents raising their children, for parents who have to keep open the lines of communication with their older children, and who have to let go of them when they are grown-up. We may pray for parents who have lost a child, and for people without children.

We may pray for the education of our children and grandchildren, for school societies and school boards, for principals, teachers, and support staff in the school, and not to be forgotten, for the students. We may pray for all study-society work that seeks to serve the Lord, for instruction by means of book and magazine, and for those giving, or receiving, that instruction. We may pray for brothers and sisters who are scientists, and for believing artists.

We may pray for today's society, in which man more and more becomes a law unto himself. We see this in the break-up of engagements, marriages and families, and in the godless attitude with respect to beginning and end of life, and in the position of man and woman in society; we also see it in the undermining of authority, lawlessness, flight into self-indulgence and drugs.

We may pray for ourselves, as children of God who have to choose daily *for* the light and against darkness in this corrupt world. We may pray for ourselves who in our choice for God's Word have to persevere against the ever-increasing pressure of public opinion, a public opinion which will increasingly think that a larger family is anti-social, that a handicapped child is an unnecessary burden, that authority in the family is an evil, that the church is antiquated, and that euthanasia is a relief.

We may pray for our nation, which is turning away from God, for our queen, our prime minister and his ministers, for the government and all its members, especially if in their official position they have to speak and make decisions as believers, we may pray for judicial and police authorities, for the army and its leaders.

We may pray for oppressed nations *and* for their oppressors, for underdeveloped nations, for the tremen-

111

dous problems of race and class, and hunger; of environment and energy supplies, for governments in the United States, Russia, China, South-Africa and in other countries.

We may pray for economic situations at home and abroad, for the task of the authorities in that area.

We may pray for employers and employees, for those who exploit and for those who are idle, for the unemployed, and for those who are comfortable in this state. We may pray for the many workers with difficult tasks, for the boys on the job and for the students, for nurses, office workers, and mechanics, who sometimes have to spend each day in an atmosphere of immorality. We may pray for the labour unions which often think in terms of revolution.

Once again it must be said that these are no more than indications to which everyone can add, expand or delete. Our *personal* prayers remain *personal*. Various things such as nature, temperament, education, age, circle of employment, time available, degree of strength and health will exert their influence. And our prayers always are and will be and remain limited. It is, therefore, a real comfort to know that not only we, but all the saints are praying, they from their side, and we from ours. And there is an infinitely greater comfort to be derived from this, that He who is sitting on the throne is omniscient. He is the allseeing One, who is always and everywhere present, whom we do not need to inform, instruct, or show the way. For before we call, He knows all things, although - happily - He does want to be asked.

Neither need we think that we have to carry the burdens of the whole world on our shoulders. We may not indifferently distantiate ourselves from them, but whatever we bring before the Lord is indeed off of our shoulders. Because of our prayers

He takes charge of all burdens and carries them on *His* shoulders.

That is benefical to us, and it is a blessing for the world, even if it neither knows nor acknowledges it.

Jas.5:16 Because it has been allotted this power, the prayer of righteous man may have great effect.

15 Thanksgiving

Where there are prayers, there is also thanksgiving.

Right?

Or is giving thanks a forgotten chapter in our life? Because this or that matter was close to our heart we may have prayed often and intently. And now the Lord has answered our prayer.

How much and in what way did we thank Him afterwards?

Where is My honour.

What is the real purpose of our existence?

We often live as if we are central. But Scripture puts us in our place by teaching us that our existence finds its aim and fulfillment in God.

This is the way it was from the beginning.

Gen.17:
And this is the way it has again become in God's covenant grace in which the LORD said to Abraham: "Walk before me and be blameless." Walk before God *again*. Be bameless as at the beginning.

Ex.19:6
God impressed this on Israel at Sinai: 'You shall be to Me a kingdom of priests and a holy nation.'

You shall be priests *again*, servants of God. You shall become a holy nation, set apart for His service.

114

1 Chron.16:4-6 David therefore appointed Levites as ministers before the ark of the LORD to continually invoke, thank, and praise the LORD, the God of Israel.

In Jeremiah, the LORD reminds His people of His honour in the sign of the waistcloth: "... As the

Jer.13:11 waistcloth clings to the loins of a man, so I made the whole house of Israel and the whole house of Judah cling to Me... that they might be for Me a

Phil.4:6 people, a name, a promise, and a glory..." Therefore the Holy Spirit says that by prayer and supplication with *thanksgiving* we must let our requests be made known to God.

Inst.3;20.28 Calvin remarks on these words that our requests are therefore, wrong and deficient when they are not accompanied by thanksgiving. We know to call upon the Lord in trouble: Father! Father!

And that is good.

Mal.1:6 But if he is a Father, then His honour may not be omitted from our mouth.

In Christ Jesus.

1 Thes.5:18 It is the will of God for us that in Christ Jesus we give thanks to Him in all circumstances. In *Christ Jesus!*

For we should not imagine that there is any merit in our thanksgiving. When we come before the throne of God with our supplications, we may do so in the name of the Lord Jesus. We may do so as if He Himself were standing behind us, encouraging us to go ahead, and speak. Speak to the Father on My authority. But what about our thanksgiving?

Can we then appear a little more freely before the Lord? Can we do so on our own authority, since, after all, we now have something to offer Him? But

115

of ourselves we never have anything to offer to the the Lord. Also with our sacrifices of praise, the fruit of our lips, that acknowledge His name, we can only appear before God's throne through Christ. If He had not fulfilled all righteousness for us, we could not place our feet anywhere before the Lord, not even in our thanksgiving. He also purifies our thanks giving, through the offering that He as our perfect high priest has brought for us once and for all.

Lost goods.

And what if we do *not* give thanks?

Is that so bad, so to speak, only because we short-change the Lord? Certainly, that too is involved, even *first* of all! For it is no small matter, easily ignored by the Lord. It is true He will forgive us if we fall short in giving thanks, but only because rather than leaving it unpunished, He has punished also that sin in His beloved Son Jesus Christ by the bitter and shameful death on the cross.

Form for Lord's Supper.

But in not giving thanks we also shortchange ourselves.

Ursinus: Comm.on H.C. 116

Ursinus says that when we fail to give thanks, we lose the goods, once given to us and we do not receive those gifts we still need and which would yet have been given to us.

That seems a strange way of putting it. Losing goods that have already been given? Does the Lord take them back?

Still it is not all that strange. For failing to give thanks means that we do not acknowledge with our whole heart that it was the Lord who gave. It means that although we have indeed received goods, we possess them in exactly the same way the world possesses.

116

The world does not acknowledge the Lord as the Giver, and hence does not thank Him. If we don't give thanks we act in precisely the same way. It is true that we possess, but we do not do so in Him. Though rich in goods we are yet poor in Him.

And if we do not repent, we will also remain poor. It may be quite possible that we do receive more goods, perhaps even after asking. But we then receive them, not in the Lord, but to our condemnation.

Then we are like the nine lepers who did not return to give God the glory. Why not? Were they not healed by the Lord Jesus? Yes, indeed, they were, but they did not see God's hand in this. They had not received their healing in faith.

Lk.17:12-19

Only the tenth one, a Samaritan, had understood the great miracle the Lord had performed in him. *He* turned back, praising God with a loud voice. And it was to *him* that the Lord said: Your *faith* has made you *well*.

Ps.51:15

> *"O LORD, open Thou my lips,*
> *and my mouth shall show forth Thy praise."*

Psalms in the night.

But when the Lord does not fulfill our most heartfelt desires, which we took to Him in fervent supplication...then what? Must we then still give thanks? Must we then give thanks because a christian must always be joyful? Does the Lord ask that from us?

Ps.39:2

He makes no unnatural, no inhuman demands does He? He knows full well and takes into account that our mouth can be dumb and silent with grief, that our soul can be bowed down.

117

Jam.5:13

*"Is any among you suffering? Let him pray.
Is any cheerful? Let him sing praise."*

Yet, through His merciful power He can give psalms in the night. Psalm 88 is a dark song in Scripture.

Ps.88:3
:5
:7
:14
:15
:16
:18

"My soul is full of troubles."
"I am like one forsaken among the dead."
"Thy wrath is heavy upon me."
"O LORD why dost Thou cast me off."
"I will suffer Thy terrors; I am helpless."
"Thy wrath has swept over me."
*"Thou hast caused lover and friend to
shun me."*
Can it get any darker?

Yet at the beginning this psalm declares God's glory.

Ps.88:1 NASB

*"O LORD, the God of my salvation,
I have cried out by day and in the night
before Thee."*
O LORD, the God of my salvation!
In spite of everything, that opening makes this song a psalm in the night.

Acts 16:22-25

Paul and Silas had been beaten with rods. With blood-covered backs, they were thrown into the inner prison, their feet fastened in stocks.

But about midnight they were praying and singing hymns to God...

Guido de Brés is about forty five years old when he is led to his death. He is still a young man, bound to life with many ties. What does he say to his fellow-prisoners?

*"Today I die for the name of God's Son.
Thanks be to God!*

I am very joyful...From moment to moment I am given strength...It is as though my Spirit has wings

118

to lift itself to heaven, where today I have been invited to the marriage feast of my Lord, of the Son of my God."!

This is also a "psalm" in the night.

Do they exist because people are such heroes of the faith?

Form for
Lord's Supper

Matt.27:46

Psalm 22:1

Ps.42:9
Form for
Lord's Supper.

No, but because our Saviour humbled Himself to the very deepest the shame and anguish of hell, when He called out with a loud voice:
"My God, My God, why hast Thou
forsaken me?"

Those are words from Psalm 22. Here they are a psalm in the darkest night the world has ever known, a night in which He held on to God's steadfast faithfulness when he said: My God. He did so that we might nevermore be forsaken of God, and so that this the song too would be with us also in the night.

Perhaps someone is thinking: I will never be able to do that, to give thanks in the night.

Do we not know our own lack of faith? Do we not know ourselves to be afraid of pain, of grief, of degeneration?

Have we not found that even small troubles upset us and make us impatient, unsatisfied, and unhappy? Do we not also notice this with other believers who start to grumble when things do not go their way?

That is true.

But the opposite is also true. In our own lives as well as in the lives of others, we sometimes see a glimpse of the wonderful grace God gives, to bear trouble. Do we thank Him for that?

119

As far as the future is concerned: no one knows it, and no one receives strength in advance. At His time, the Lord gives grace to live while we live.

He also at His time gives grace to die when we die. Grace to suffer, to bear grief, to suffer persecution, to grow old. He does this at His time, and according to His good pleasure.

But He does not give it automatically, without our asking. Big words in advance do not suit us. But life with the Lord, today, in the situation as it is right now, that is what we should seek. Not only when things start happening to us, when things are going wrong, but now. And then today we may also ask Him to take charge of us in the future.

Ps.71:17-18

> "*O God, from my youth*
> *Thou hast taught me,*
> *and I still proclaim*
> *Thy wondrous deeds.*
> *So even to old age and grey hairs,*
> *O God, do not forsake me...*"

Ps.88:1

Ask Him now today: that we may live in the firm faith that He, the God of our salvation, will do it.

Always give thanks

When shall we give thanks to God?

Only when we have received something from Him in answer to our prayer?

Of course, then too.

Phil.4:6

But Scripture says that with thanksgiving we must let our requests be made known to God. This means that we are to give thanks not only after we have received something, but immediately while we are asking.

That is a fitting attitude for us before the Lord.

H.C. 129

For, in the first place, if we pray according to God's Word, do we not say in faith, amen? Amen means it shall truly and surely be. It means that the Lord has much more certainly heard my prayer than I feel in my heart that I desire this of Him. Since this is so, our faith may also be shown in giving thanks in advance for the answer that will certainly come, not in a forced way, but trusting in God's promises, after having listened carefully to His Word. (chapter 9 & 11)

Matt.15:36

Acts 27:35

And further, does the Lord not surround us day by day with His care? The Lord Jesus gave thanks for bread, as did Paul. God created foods to be received with thanksgiving. Foods only?

1 Tim.4:3-4

What about clothing, shelter, environment?

Acts 28:15
Matt.6:25-34

Paul gives thanks when, after years of imprisonment and after a difficult journey, he meets the brethren in Italy.

Food, drink, clothing, meeting each other - these are all very ordinary things. But God's hand is in them, and He is not too far removed from us to be thanked for such things.

Acts 17:28

"In Him we live and move and have our being." There is never one moment that He does not surround us, and that He does not lay His hands upon us.

Ps.139:5

Whether in traffic, at our job, in our housework, in church, in the swimming pool, in the airplane, whether we are sleeping, or lying awake, in health, in feverish dreams, when we are nervous, sad, or happy, when our mind is keen and clear, or when we become demented, when we are anaesthetised, or when we are in a coma, or in the hour of our death,

Ps.139:18

He is with us and when we awake - from the sleep of death - I am still with Him.

In the previous chapter we have mentioned quite a number of things for which we may pray. Is there one single thing or situation for which or in which our thanks for God's goodness is not fitting?

Fearfulness

H.C.27

But doesn't this make for frightened, fearful people, who must always be afraid that ever and again they fall short in thankfulness? Does not faith in God's almighty and ever present power, whereby as with His hand, He still upholds heaven and earth and our life-does that faith not become a rod, always and forever driving us on?

No, this is not the way it is.

In chapter 6 we have seen that our prayer is not an information service, through which we need to keep God informed. The same is true for our thanksgiving. Do we have a bird's eye view of all that we receive from the Lord?

No finite creature can ever totally and continually keep that before his mind's eye, let alone express it all verbally in prayers of thanksgiving. Not even angels can do that for they too are finite creatures. Adam could not do it, not even *before* the fall. The Lord does not ask that of us. And we, after our fall into sin, we cannot even come close to doing it at all. Of ourselves, we do not see any of it any more. Of ourselves, we do not want to see the hand of God at *all*.

But what has happened?

There has been the miracle of a new birth. Our ears, which were deaf, can hear again. Our blinded eyes can see again. Our dead heart can understand again, and so takes up the melody and the teaching of Psalm 103:

Ps.103:22

> *"Bless the LORD, all His works,*
> *in all places of His dominion.*
> *Bless the LORD, O my soul!"*

Yes, it is true, we do so imperfectly.

Undoubtedly, the sound is too meager.

Ps.103:13 NASB

Ps.40:8 &
Heb.10:5-10

H.C.60

But no one needs to go around with guilt feelings because of that.For the LORD has had compassion on us as a father has compassion on his children. He has given us a mediator, who kept God's law, the law of thankfulness, in His heart. And he has done so as a surety, a ransom and a substitute - as if we ourselves had fulfilled all the thankfulness that He has fulfilled for us.

1) G. Groen Prinsterer, Handboek der Geschiedenis van het Vaderland. 1927.

16 The Labour of Prayer

Prayer does not just happen automatically. We do not always find it easy.

We sometimes speak of "praying and working", the one activity next to the other. But praying in itself is working. Often we have to *force* ourselves to the labour of prayer.

Although He was the Son.

Matt.3:17 a.o. No man has ever had a more intimate relationship with the Father than the Lord Jesus. He was the Son of the Father.

Jn.10:30 He could say to the Jews: "I and the Father are one." There was never anything separating Him from the Father. He always delighted to do God's will. God's law was within His heart. If ever anyone was able to *Ps.40:9* go in and out of the heavenly palace unhindered, it was Him. And what do we read about Him?

Mk.1:35 This: "And in the morning, a *great while before day*, He rose and went out to a lonely place, and there He prayed."

Matt.14:23 And this: "And after He had dismissed the crowds, He went up on the mountain by Himself to pray." This was after the report of the death of John the *Jn.4:6* Baptist, a message that would have shocked Him. It was also after a long day of hard work among the *Mk.4:38* crowds. He was in need of rest, of sleep. He could

124

sleep through a storm after a heavy day.

But the need for communion with the Father was stronger in Him. For that He put everything else aside. Crowds and disciples He sent away.

Jn.6:15 He withstood them in their enthusiasm to make Him king. He did not consider weariness and need of sleep, but withdrew to a mountain. For the greater part of the night, He wanted to be alone.

Lk.6:12 Sometimes He wanted to be alone for a whole night. Who can avoid thinking of Gethsemane, in this connection?

Matt.26:38-39 Being sorrowful and very troubled He desired the sympathy of His disciples: "Remain here, and watch with Me." But He withdrew Himself from their supporting company and went into the "inner room" of the garden, there to put His supplication before *Heb.5:8* the face of the Father. And so He, although He was *Rom.8:7* the Son, has set Himself to pray. What about us who are by nature hostile to God? Of ourselves we cannot *Heb.12:1 NAS* and will not submit to God's law. Sin so easily *Rom.7:23* entangles us. And in our heart Satan finds us captives to the laws of sin.

How necessary it must be for *us*, then, to *set* ourselves to pray, How necessary it must be for us to cling to God's promises.

Decrees

The Lord knows this full well. Therefore He did not leave it entirely up to the people of the Old Covenant where and how often they wanted to pray to Him. He came to the aid of Israel with decrees, in which He asked for the dedication of His people.

Ex.23:17	Thus all the males had to appear before the LORD three times a year in the sanctuary, on the great feast day.
1 Sam.1:3	Elkanah used to go up year after year to worship and to sacrifice to the LORD at Shiloh.
Lk.2:41	Joseph and Mary went to Jerusalem every year at the feast of Passover. These were no holiday trips. From Nazareth to Jerusalem, via the upper Jordan region, was a journey of some 130 to 150 km. Such a journey, there and back, in those times and with the means of transportation then available, and added to that the stay in Jerusalem - what dedication that must have required. What preparation! Whoever did not absolutely want to call upon the Lord in His sanctuary would really not have bothered and would have stayed home.

Further, the LORD gave rules for the Sabbath, the new moon, and the day of atonement. Not all of these would have had the same great inpact on the usual course of daily life, but all positively required the dedicated commitment of the people.

Certainly, Israel could also present freewill offerings. Not the whole of the service of the LORD was laid down in decrees and regulations. But in addition to the freewill ones, there were still the regulatory daily sacrifices. There were the daily morning and evening sacrifices, Further, there were extra sacrifices on the Sabbath and other feastdays. There was the daily fragant incense offering. All of these called God's people and helped them maintain communion with the LORD, and *set* them to achieve it.

Custom.

In this way good customs were formed in the god-fearing family, and they were a help in life with the LORD.

Lk.4:6 There was the custom of keeping the Sabbath. Although he was the Son, the Lord Jesus did not scorn but maintained the Sabbath.

Dan.6:10 Daniel went down upon his knees three times a day and gave thanks before his God.

We can think of the psalmist:
Ps.55:17 *"Evening and morning and at noon*
I utter my complaint and moan..."

These words show regularity and custom.

Acts 3:1 Peter and John went up to the temple at the hour of prayer, following a fixed pattern.

Acts 10:30 Cornelius tells Peter that he was keeping the ninth hour of prayer.

There was a regular time for a regular custom.

We no longer have regulations as they were under the Old Covenant. But we have been able to take over the custom of Sunday observance. Then we go to church. We set ourselves to do that. And if all is right we dedicate ourselves to it.

At fixed times, according to custom, we celebrate the Lord's Supper in the congregation.

The Scriptures speak of giving thanks at mealtimes. Building on that, our fathers adopted the custom of praying, reading the Scripture, and giving thanks at meals. We still reap the benefit of that custom. Modern life makes family ties less close than they used to be. It has therefore become difficult to keep up the custom of family devotions. But it will be worthwhile for us to devote ourselves to their preservation both for our own sake, and for the sake of our

127

children - that the lord may be praised and thanked in our families.

In such customs our faith life finds support and stimulation. And also in our prayer life the custom may exist to go into the inner room, and to *set* ourselves to call upon the Lord in the *labour* of prayer.

Preparation.

How?

Do we simply enter into the heavenly palace, without having any idea of what we will say to the Lord. Do we prepare ourselves? When we have to go and see the doctor, we think about what we will say. We want to present our complaints as clearly as we can. Should we appear before the Lord with less preparation?

Ps.147:9   O, sure, He hears the inarticulate cries of the young raven. He also hears our crying and sighing to Him when words fail us. But in the normal course of our life, may we stay at cries and sighs? Or do we first set our minds to thinking about the sins we must confess and about our sinful nature, which we cannot put off? Do we first think about the how and what of our needs and troubles in the family, in our work, in sickness, in anxiety?

And do we then consciously take hold of the promises God has given us, and come to Him on the basis of those promises?

Routine and thoughtlessness are deadly enemies to our prayer life. But when we reverently prepare to meet God in habitual prayer, then there is life.

1 Tim.2:1-2   We also pray for others. We make intercession for the church and for the world. And so we should.

Everyone who sets himself to that task discovers something. He discovers that the sphere of his intercession becomes wider and wider. It expands across oceans and continents. He discovers more people, more things, more needs all the time, for which we must call on the Lord.

It can - and does! happen that this sphere becomes *so* wide that eventually we can no longer see the whole of it. It can happen that we forget someone, whom we had definitely promised to pray for. It can happen that certain matters fall outside the attention of our prayer, although we had *so* positively resolved to bring them before the Lord continually. With a shock we can come to the realization that we have fallen short.

And we are ashamed.

If that happens, would there be anything against making and keeping up a well-considered list of people and things for which we pray? That *too* can be a part of the labour of prayer.

And if that list becomes long-and it will, would there be anything against making a simple schedule, for a week, or longer to pray for these things on Monday, for those people on Tuesday, and on Wednesday for other things or persons, and so on?

Because of our reverence for Him, and for the sake of others as well as ourselves, we cannot just talk away at random when we stand before God's throne.

Fasting and prayer.

Preparation, dedication, custom: these are not in conflict with Scripture. That is also clear from the common Biblical expression: fasting and prayer.

Fasting means not eating, or sometimes, eating very soberly.

Is.58:3 Why did people do this? The answer is that it was a sign of humbling oneself.

Lev.16:29:31 Once a year on the day of Atonement, the Israelites had to fast.

1 Sam.7:5-6
2 Sam.12:16

Ps.35:13 NASB
Ezra 8:23 In addition, there was voluntary fasting in Israel. Samuel prayed for the people, and they fasted that day. David besought the LORD for the life of his child, and he fasted. In Psalm 35 David says that he humbled his soul with fasting and prayer. Ezra writes: So we fasted and besought our God. We read of Manasseh, Nehemiah and Daniel that they fasted and prayed.

Lk.2:37
Matt.17:21

Acts 13:3 Anna worshiped God with fasting and prayer. "But this kind never comes out except by prayer and fasting", says the Lord Jesus when his disciples could not cast out a demon. After fasting and prayer Paul and Barnabas are sent out by the church at Antioch to preach the gospel.

What does this have to do with our prayer? After all, we no longer fast.

No, we no longer fast. Nevertheless, we can learn from it that prayer requires preparation and dedication. People had to set themselves to fasting. It didn't happen automatically, but needed perseverance. And it was done in preparation for prayer.

Whether the strength of our prayer has increased now that we no longer fast is an open question. But we should at least know the purpose of it, namely, *dedication*, *preparation* and *humbling*.

Spontaneous prayer.

Is there not any room for spontaneity in our relationship with the Lord, for prayer straight from the heart, according to the need of the moment? There is, indeed, much room and every opportunity for that. How could it be otherwise in a *living* relationship? The life of faith may find support in dedication, habit and preparation - but it is not made of rules and regulations.

Lev.7:11-15

Thus, in addition to the prescribed offerings, Israel had her freewill peace offerings. To give thanks to the LORD she had the thank offering. To praise the LORD she had the praise offering. To make a vow to the LORD she had the votive offering. To express

Lev.22:18

total surrender to Him she had the burnt offering.

Gen.28:20

After his dream at Bethel, Jacob made a vow to the LORD.

Judg.11:30

Jephthah did the same before he began the battle for the people of God.

1 Sam.1:11

When she poured out her heart before the LORD, Hannah made a vow that, if He would give her a son, she would give him to the LORD.

Num.6:1-21

An Israelite could separate himself to the LORD for any period of time by the vow of the Nazarite.

Ps.66:13-14

> *"I will come into Thy house*
> *with burnt offerings;*
> *I will pay Thee my vows,*
> *that which my lips uttered*
> *and my mouth promised*
> *when I was in trouble."*

Acts 18:18
NASB

We read of Paul that he was keeping a vow.

Acts 21:23

In the church of Jerusalem there are four men who

131

were under a vow. In life with the LORD there is most certainly much room for a living, fluid, spontaneous relationship, also where prayer is concerned. The Scriptures speak of people perishing of hunger and thirst, who cried to God in their trouble. It speaks of people who drew near to the gates of death, of those who were caught in a storm at sea and reeled and staggered like drunken men. That was crying in the need of the moment. There was no time for consideration and preparation. Nor was this needed. The troubled heart cried to God as the drowning screamed for help.

Ps.107:1-32   "And He delivered them from their distress."

Acts 3:8   The lame man at the Beautiful Gate, who had been healed through the word of Peter, stood up and walked and entered the temple with the apostles, "walking and leaping and praising God." The man could not contain himself. He had had no oportunity to prepare himself. But of that which his heart was full, his mouth had to give expression to in that hour of prayer.

Heb.13:15   The Lord created life. He gave His people rules by which to live. But he also delights in our voluntary, spontaneous praise as the fruit of lips that acknowledge His name.

Prayer by impulse.

We may have experienced a short and quick prayer by impulse. It is not an expression very often used among us. Yet it is to be hoped that it *is* practised among us, not in the sense of a short hasty little prayer that must quickly get us out of trouble, for that is not even deserving of the name prayer. But there is another possiblity. In times of need, in sorrow, when we receive a heavy blow, in joy, when our heart is filled with thankfulness, then the heart can be touched and can rise to God on the wings of only a few words. It can happen at work, or just before an operation. It can happen on an anniversary, or on the mountain top with a magnificent view, or it can happen behind the wheel of the car. A person with a matter-of-fact nature will send such a prayer less frequently than a more emotional one. But in countless instances such prayers may have a place in our living relationship with the LORD.

But does the fact that it is unprepared and not premeditated mean that it is also thoughtless?

Certainly not.

Neh.2:4

For it only sprouts up on the field of our daily walk with God. If in Nehemiah 2:4 we are dealing with a "prayer by impulse" - and it looks that way - then that was no shallow little prayer to get Nehemiah out of trouble. No, it sprouted from the soil of Nehemiah's struggle of faith for the people and land and city of the promise, a struggle which speaks to us in the well thought-out and well prepared prayer of chapter 1:5-11.

Neh.1:5-11

The same goes for the other short prayers of this man of God, who burnt himself out in the service of God and in doing that maintained a continuing living contact with his LORD. See ch. 4:4-5; 5:19; and the verses 14, 22 and 29, 31 of the last chapter. See also the well thought-out, balanced construction of the prayer of 9:6-37, which indicates the basis of the shorter prayers.

Neh.4:4-5

Neh.5:19

Neh.9:6-37

Prayer without words.

Even without words the heart can be lifted up to God. This can happen in all kinds of circumstances and does not necessarily mean that there is, or has been, no work of prayer. Sometimes there has been a lifetime of such work.

Scriptures give examples of that too.

Ps.38:13
NASB
David, overcome by difficulties and grief says in Psalm 38: "I am like a dumb man who does not open his mouth."

And in Psalm 39:
Ps.39:9 NASB
> *"I have become dumb,*
> *I do not open my mouth."*

Ps.62:1,6
NASB
His soul waits in silence for God alone. This does not mean that he will simply cease praying from now on. The Marginal Notes put it so beautifully: when it says that it is as if in Ps.62:1 the text were saying: "whatever happens, I will not cease in prayer and faith to expect God's salvation and help..."

Ezra 9
And Ezra, on hearing of the mixed marriages in Israel so shortly after the return from exile, sat appalled for a whole day. Words failed him. But he did lift up his soul to God in the work of prayer. And the torrent of his prayer broke loose.

Ps.62:1
So also a song of praise to God can be sung in silence, in silence because of overwhelming thankfulness.

It can happen that all things have been brought before the Lord and that our soul has become quiet before Him, while there is yet the need to stay with the Lord, as a weaned child with his mother, consciously and purposefully seeking refuge with Him.

Ps.131
We can also be so depressed, so confused and disturbed by sickness, fever, sorrow, tension, fear, and fatigue, - that we are no longer able to form words and phrases. Then the soul can only lift itself to God with sighing. As an elderly brother uttered with extreme difficulty: "I can no longer...pray for others... or for myself...only sigh..." If that hap-

134

pens to be the case with us at some point, should we then fear that our way is hidden from the Lord?

Ps.102:20
Mk.7:34

Rom.8:26,27

No. For He hears the groans of the prisoners. The Lord Jesus sighed to God for the need of a deaf-mute... And because we do not know how to pray as we ought, the Holy Spirit Himself intercedes for us with sighs too deep for words. And He who searches the hearts, knows what is the mind of the spirit.

Not an eloquent man.

Ex.4:10

God creates each man according to His high purpose. One is able to clearly put into words what goes on inside him, while another, like Moses, is not an eloquent man. Would the prayer of the eloquent be pleasing to the Lord because of its abundance of words, and not that of the halting speaker because it is produced with such difficulty?

Ex.4:11

But who made man's mouth? Is it not He, the LORD?

That goes for the praying mouth, too!

But if someone is afraid of work, and finds it too much trouble to ask himself what to put before the Lord and in what manner he should do so - if *that* is the reason he has no words - then a drying wind will blow across the field of his prayer life. And even if he were able to cover this desert with the most flowery language, he would be unable to bring it to bloom.

But he who, while struggling with his words, humbly approaches God, he is no less than the supplicant who has received the gift of eloquence. Both lie helpless and needy before the throne of the God of life. The words of their prayer do not offer any

135

Ps.139:5,10   support. The only thing which provides a sure grip
is the hand of the LORD.

Ps.123:2   "Behold, as the eyes of the servants
look to the hand of their master,
as the eyes of a maid
to the hand of her mistress,"
so the eyes of the one as well as the other may look
to the LORD their God.

1 Sam.16:7   For God's hand alone can serve. And He looks to
the heart that lifts itself up in prayer to Him.

17 Prayer In Adversity

Because we are praying in enemy territory and are opposed by the enemy, prayer demands our attention. To the devil it would be worth everything if we were to weaken in prayer, or even to stop altogether. It would be worth everything to him if we would no longer seek out God's promises, and draw the Lord to us so He may indeed show us His help. It would be worth everything to him if we were to become withered branches.

Jn.15:1-8

Satan-adversary.

So Satan, whose name means adversary, tries to keep us from praying.

How does he do this?

1 Pet. 5:8
Gen.3:1

He will use any means, the ordinary as well as the seemingly pious. He prowls around like a roaring lion, but also as a sly tempter. And we, are we watchful? Do we still reckon with his opposition? Or do we consider it a somewhat outdated point of view, even if we don't care to say this out loud? And is that perhaps one reason why satan finds it so easy to attack us in our spiritual barrenness, in our slowness, and in our carelessness in our walk with the Lord?

137

Everyday opposition.

We are about to pray personally. Now this very night, we will go into our inner room to pray.

But...did we switch off the headlights of the car? It would be awful to be stuck with a dead battery in the morning!

We are about to pray. But...it is just time for the news. And, after all, we must keep ourselves informed.

Or, just when we are about to pray we realize that we have not even looked at today's paper. And we should be involved. So we better read the paper first, and then...

Or, this letter here really must be posted. Then it will still catch tonight's mail.

Or, we receive a phone call. It is a business relation. There is an appointment for a meeting, or for a birthday. And such calls tend to drag on.

Or...

Everyone can fill in something that applies to himself. All these are innocent, very ordinary, everyday things, which, however, are skillfully used by the adversary to keep us from praying. And, to be honest, are we ourselves not also to blame? Going into the inner room requires dedication. Really, how strong is our desire to talk to the Lord?

There is also another possibility.

We are about to pray. But as soon as we start thinking about it, we feel tired. After all, it was late last night. We are sleeply. We cannot keep our minds on prayer. And even if we *do* feel fine, we do not live under a yoke of slavery, do we? Surely we do not necessarily have to pray *so* often and *for so* long?

And what do we do? We say some familiar words. The Lord's prayer for instance. It is a short prayer and is it not *always* good? It's the perfect prayer, isn't it?

And so we are finished.

We have prayed.

So we think.

But...have we even crossed the threshold of the heavenly palace?

Perhaps someone finds it improper to connect prayer life with such common, everyday things. But is it not better to frankly discuss them with each other, rather than pretending to be above flesh and blood and an inert spirit?

Matt.9:13
Zech.12:10
Lk.11:13

If we admit and confess what the situation is concerning us and our prayer life, if we learn to see our *sin* in this - then there is hope! Then we may remember that the Lord Jesus did not come to call the righteous, but sinners to repentance. Despite the poverty of our prayer life, there are the firm promises that He will hear. "If you then, who are evil, know how to give good gifts to your children, how much more will the heavenly Father give the Holy Spirit to those who ask Him!"

Talking to ourself.

There is another, more subtle way in which Satan can oppose us.

Matt.6:6

When we want to pray we go into the "inner room," and that is good and necessary.

139

But we do not go there to have a *little talk with ourselves*. Not when we think, whisper, or perhaps even speak out loud. To whom actually are we speaking? To ourselves? It is very true that we can be doing that! But in that situation we are like someone who shoots without an aim. If we do not direct ourselves to *God*, if we do not draw nigh to *Him*, if our prayer is just talking without finding its goal in Him, the living God, then our prayer simply does not get any further than the walls of our existence. Then our prayer is simply a monologue. It may perhaps be a religious monologue, but it is not seeking God's ear which is inclined to us. When this happens, Satan has indeed succeeded in blocking our communion with the Lord. He makes use of a wrong attitude of ours which cripples the wings of our prayer, with the result that our expectations are not eagerly directed *towards* the hearing and listening to the Lord, who wants to respond to our prayer for our good.

We really must go *out* to God, cleaving to His promises, and pour out our hearts to Him.

Prayer is not automatic.

"Pious" resistance.

Not automatic?

This is where Satan enters his "pious" weapons into the battle.

Is prayer not automatic? Do we have to set ourselves to pray; and make an effort; make it a habit; prepare ourselves; Do we need to make notes, or even a schedule?

Surely that is pure ritualism! What has become of "real" prayer?

Is it not so that you only have "real" prayer when you feel the *need* for it? After all, does it not in this way come straight from the *heart*? But just like the image of the ideal-Christian(ch.12), so the image of "real", ideal prayer can be harmful. Satan measures our prayers by that ideal image, and we happily go along with him! For we are wide open to those super-pious, but unscriptural ideals.

And if our prayers are measured by those, then they are not nearly up to par. Our prayer will never work the way it is supposed to according to the ideal. Never in a lifetime will it be what the ideal says it should be. The demands are always too high. Our prayer accomplishments are always lacking. Then we never dare to hope for answers to prayer. How could we? Our expectation fades away. Our prayers fall silent.

And the adversary has reached his goal. By such pious-seeming means.

False antithesis.

But it is not pious and it is not scriptural.

Shouldn't our prayer be a matter of heart and need?

It certainly should. What kind of prayer would it be, if we put ourselves before God's throne and address Him, while thinking to ourselves: I really have no need to do this?

But how can anyone think that dedication, habit and preparation on the one hand, and heartfelt need on the other, have to be mutually exclusive?

Young people who fall in love know better than that. They need to get to know each other. Their hearts go out to each other. Then what do they do? They go all out to get to know other. They make it a habit of getting together on the weekends. And they would

141

be very surprised if someone were to tell them that because their relationship is a habit and because they make an effort for it, that it isn't a matter of the heart.

That is one way of looking at the matter.

But the following consideration is much more important. Where does the Bible teach us that it was not a matter of the heart when according to custom, Isreal set herself to attend the great feast days? Where does the Bible teach that there was no need involved, and no heartfelt joy in being allowed to meet God?

The songs of pilgrimage-Psalm 120-134- tell us an altogether different story:

Ps.122:1
> *"I was glad when they said to me:*
> *'Let us go to the house of the LORD'."*

Dan.6:11
Where does Scripture say that Daniel's heart remained cold when he, as was his custom, bent his knees three times a day and praised his God? Where does it

Lk.4:16
say that when the Lord Jesus as was His custom, went to the synagogue on the sabbath that He did not do so from the heart?

Mk.1:35
Where does it say - and a terrible thought it is - that His heart was not invovled when He took the trouble to get up in the middle of the night to go up on the mountain to pray?

Where does it say that He did not cry from the depths of His heart when He *intentionally* withdrew Himself

Matt.26:39
into the garden of Gethsemane to pray to the Father with tears?

Nowhere does Scripture teach these things. It does teach us, however, that under the old dispensation

142

the LORD Himself gave precepts and ordinances, by which customs developed and had to develop in Israel.

We must be dedicated - from the heart.

We must prepare ourselves because of pressing needs.

We must form habits and customs-because our heart urges us to do so. And we must never let ourselves be pushed away from the throne of God by a seemingly pious, but false antitheses, which Satan uses to keep us from praying.

Accuser.

In the prophecies of Zechariah we read how Satan is bent on destroying the relationship between the LORD and His people.

The LORD had brought Israel back from Babylonia.

What joy!

Ps.126:1 NASB
"When the LORD brought back the captive ones of Zion, we were like those who dream."

Ezra 3
Israel could hardly believe it, it was *so* wonderful. With great enthusiasm the people started to rebuild the temple.

Hag.1:4&9
But quite quickly this enthusiasm started to wane. The people kept building their own houses, but they left the temple in ruins for more than ten years.

Hag.1:12-14
Then as a result of Haggai's preaching the LORD brought about a new obedience. Israel saw its sin and once again started to work on the rebuilding of God's house.

Zech.3:1-10
Then another prophet, Zechariah, was sent to comfort the people. In a vision he saw Joshua the high priest standing before the angel of the LORD. And

143

then he saw something terrible. As were the people so was the high priest, it seemed. As there was a neglectful people, so there was an unclean priest. For Joshua is clothed with filthy garments!

Ex.40:13

And who is that, standing beside him? It is Satan! And what does he do? He accuses Joshua. He points at those filthy clothes. Must such a priest make atonement for *such* a people? Can that be possible? Has not the LORD Himself made it known that *that* was not the way He wanted it?

So Satan can also accuse us.

He can point out our sins to us and rightly so. He can point to ugly sins which make us detestable before God. And who can say how often we have fallen into them already and will fall again?

How then shall we still be able to pray?

He can rightly point to our sinful nature. Even if at night we would not be able to pinpoint one single sin, even then, did we really love the Lord above all and our neighbour as ourself? And yet we *still* pray?

He can accuse us of not being fervent in prayer, of not longing to meet with God with real desire, of not being able to do without the props of preparation and custom. And rightly so. And do we then still have the nerve to approach God? He can rightly confront us with the fact that our faith in God is so weak and that we just cannot shake unbelief and lack of faith. And then do we still dare to take the liberty of appearing before God's throne?

H.C.129

He can rightly sneer that our *amen* is so listless, that sometimes we hardly believe that the Lord heard us, let alone that we expect in faith that He much more certainly hears our prayer than we feel in our heart that we desire this of Him.

And then do we still call on Him?

So Satan accuses us. How will we dare raise heart and hand to the Holy One?

A liar from the beginning.

Jn.8:44

However, although Satan can say things that are true, he never speaks the *truth*, that is, God's truth. He is a liar as he has always been. His half truths are whole lies. For God is indeed holy. That is why there is no Saviour like Him, (chapter 3.) A Saviour who pulled Joshua out of the fire of exile like a piece of wood.

Zech.3:4

Zach.3:8

He is holy. That is why He does great things for His people. When Joshua is defenceless, He rebukes Satan and says: "Remove the filthy garments from him...I have taken your iniquity away from you." He is holy. That is why He promises: "Behold, I will bring my servant the Branch", who will be a priest, and the Lamb of God that takes away the sin of the world.

H.C.60

Thus the LORD Himself rebukes the accuser of priest and people.

Lord's Supper Form.

And although my conscience accuses me that I have grievously sinned against all God's commandments, and have never kept any of them; and although I do not serve God with such zeal as He requires; and although I must admit that I have no defence against any of Satan's accusations concerning me; yet from the depths I may call upon the Holy One of Israel:

Ps.130:3-8

> *"If Thou, O LORD, shouldest mark iniquities,*
> *LORD, who could stand?*
> *But there is forgiveness with Thee,*
> *that Thou mayest be feared.*

I wait for the LORD, my soul waits,
and in His Word I hope;
my soul waits for the LORD
more than watchmen for the morning,
O Israel, hope in the LORD!
For with the LORD there is steadfast love,
and with Him is plenteous redemption.
And He will redeem Israel
from all his iniquities."

And along the stages of God's steadfast promises I may ascend to His throne and reverently address Him. For: "God is not a man, that He should lie, or a son of man, that He should repent. Has He said and will He not do it? Or has He spoken, and will He not fulfill it?"

Num.23:19

This is He, who said to His covenant people:
"Call upon Me in the day of trouble;
I will deliver you,
*   and you shall glorify Me."*

Ps.50:15